A Basic Income
POCKETBOOK

ANNIE MILLER

Luath Press Limited
EDINBURGH
www.luath.co.uk

First published 2020

ISBN: 978-1-912147-62-5

The paper used in this book is recyclable.
It is made from low chlorine pulps
produced in a low energy, low emissions
manner from renewable forests.

Printed and bound by
Ashford Colour Press, Gosport

Typeset in 10.5 point Din by 3btype.com

The author's right to be identified as
author of this work under the Copyright,
Designs and Patents Act 1988 has been
asserted.

© Annie Miller

ANNIE MILLER, now retired, spent the major part of her working life as an academic economist at Heriot-Watt University in Edinburgh.

In 1986, Annie was a co-founder of the international Basic Income European/Earth Network (BIEN). In 1984, she was a co-founder of the Basic Income Research Group (BIRG), which became the Citizen's Basic Income Trust (CBIT) in 2017. Annie has been a trustee since 1989 and is currently its Chair. She contributes regularly to its *Citizen's Income Newsletter*. In 2016, she also co-founded the Citizen's Basic Income Network Scotland (CBINS). She gives talks to groups around the UK, and has presented papers on BI at conferences both here in the UK and abroad. Her first book, *A Basic Income Handbook*, was published in 2017.

Annie became a member of the Religious Society of Friends (Quakers) in 1978. Her faith, her belief in 'that of God in everyone', and her commitment to the Quaker testimonies (values) of peace, equality, integrity and simplicity inspire all her work.

A beautifully concise yet competent and comprehensive introduction to basic income by one of the founding members of the international basic income movement.
PHILIPPE VAN PARIJS, Chair of BIEN's International Advisory Board

This is an amazingly comprehensive and helpful little book. In particular, the methodology for designing and costing basic income schemes, and the practical DIY templates to do this, will be very valuable for NGOs, trade unions and political parties. It's also a good overview of very recent thinking about basic income during the last decade.
DR ANNE GRAY, economist/social policy researcher and visiting Fellow at London South Bank University

Annie Miller's engaging account of the theory and practice of basic income has all the markings of a key source for this highly topical approach to income inequality.
GREG MICHAELSON, Emeritus Professor of Computer Science, Heriot-Watt University.

By the same author:

Essentials of Basic Income (2020) Edinburgh: Luath Press

A Basic Income Handbook (2017) Edinburgh: Luath Press

Mair, D. and Miller, A. (Eds) (1991). *A Modern Guide to Economic Thought: An Introduction to Comparative Schools of Thought in Economics.* Aldershot: Edward Elgar

HAIKU

individual, unconditional, universal happiness.

Contents

List of Figures	11
List of Tables	12
List of Abbreviations	14
A note about terminology	16
Preface	21
Acknowledgements	28

PART I   MEANS AND ENDS

Chapter 1   **Values and vision**   30
    Imagine...   30
    What sort of society do we wish to create for ourselves and for future generations?   31
    Justification for a BI system   33
    The case for vertical redistribution of income from rich to poor   35
    Who are the rich?   36

Chapter 2   **What is wrong with the current UK Social Security system?**   38
    The National Insurance (NI) system   38
    Structural faults in the Social Assistance system   40
    Would an improved NI and SA system be achievable in the UK?   44

Chapter 3   **The generic basic income**   47
    What is a basic income?   47
    What broad objectives could a basic income help to fulfil?   51
    How do the defining characteristics of a basic income help to fulfil the objectives?   53

	Criticisms of the characteristics of the generic basic income	60
PART II	**BI SCHEMES AND PILOT EXPERIMENTS FROM AROUND THE WORLD**	
Chapter 4	**BI pilot projects from North America**	64
	Mincome program, Dauphin, Manitoba, Canada, 1974–9	64
	Alaska, 1976–present	67
Chapter 5	**Namibia and Iran**	70
	Namibia, 2008–9	70
	Iran, 2010–6	72
Chapter 6	**India's BI pilot experiments, 2011–13**	76
Chapter 7	**Some recent BI experiments and proposals**	83
	Finland, 2017–8	83
	Scotland, 2017–present	85
	Kenya, 2017–30	86
	Republic of Korea, 2019–present	87
PART III	**PRACTICAL ISSUES: DESIGNING AND COSTING A BASIC INCOME MODEL**	
Chapter 8	**Designing a BI model:**	90
	How much of the UK Social Security system could a BI replace?	91
	Eligibility and migration	93
	Poverty-prevention benchmarks	95
	At what levels should the BIs be set?	99
	Full BIs	100
	Treatment of NI benefits	102
	Treatment of Social Assistance Benefits	104
	Examples of a BI scheme for a fully fiscally-devolved Scotland and for the UK	107

Chapter 9	**Administrative matters**	111
	Co-ordinated or integrated benefit-and-income-tax-systems?	111
	Setting up a database	112
	Delivery	113
	Indexation	114
	Implementation	114
	Redeployment of redundant civil servants	115
Chapter 10	**Sources of finance to fund a BI model**	117
	Potential sources of finance for a BI model	117
	Tax revenues, Social Security expenditure and tax expenditures	119
	Why income tax is the best source of finance for BIs	124
	The proposed restructured income tax system	125
	A method for costing a BI model financed by a restructured income tax system	128
	Parallel income tax schedules – an earnings or income disregard	131
Chapter 11	**Who says we can't afford an adequate BI system?**	133
	How much would a small Personal Allowance cost in terms of lost income tax revenue?	133
	Approximate cost of a model with the same full BI for all adults	135
	How to calculate the breakeven points between a BI model and the current income tax schedule	136
PART IV	**WHERE NEXT?**	
Chapter 12	**Economic effects of BI**	148
	Work incentive effects and labour supply	148

	Basic Income and the British Trades Unions	149
	The business case for BI	151
	Macroeconomic effects of BI	153
Chapter 13	**The anatomy of basic income pilot experiments**	157
	Microsimulation models and pilot experiments	157
	BI pilot experiments	162
	The planning stage	163
	The implementation stage	167
	Later stages	169
	The costs of a basic income pilot experiment	169
Chapter 14	**Conclusion**	172
	The nature of criticism of BI	172
	The political process	175
	How might the BI model to be implemented be chosen?	178
	Hope for the future	180

APPENDICES

Appendix A	Data for the UK and Scotland, 2017–19	184
Appendix B	WORK BOOK: Design and cost your own BI model	188
Appendix C	Excel template for designing and costing your own BI model.	193
Appendix D	Chronology of basic income with respect to the UK	198
Appendix E	*'Aye, but…'*	210

Main sources of data	220
Select Bibliography	226
Organisations (Information and Contacts)	232
Index	235

List of Figures

Figure 11.1　Two basic income models compared with the 2020–21 UK income tax schedules　　139

List of Tables

Table 3.1	How the defining characteristics of a basic income help to fulfil the broad objectives	54
Table 3.2	The structure of income maintenance systems	58
Table 8.1	EU official poverty benchmarks for the UK, based on the couple	96
Table 8.2	A new poverty benchmark for the UK, based on the individual	98
Table 8.3	Single pensioner benefit levels	103
Table 8.4	Costs of the components of the margin for 2020–21, based on data available in 2019	106
Table 8.5 Scot	Cost of a sample BI model for Scotland in 2020–21	108
Table 8.5 UK	Cost of a sample BI model for the UK in 2020–21	108
Table 8.6	BIs by household type, using the example for Scotland	110
Table 10.1	Tax revenues, Social Security expenditure and costs of tax expenditures for the UK	121
Table 10.2 Scot	Method for costing a BI model for Scotland in 2020–21	128
Table 10.2 UK	Method for costing a BI model for the UK in 2020–21	129
Table 11.1	A method for estimating the approximate cost of models that give full BIs to all adults	135

Table 11.2 UK	Tax schedules, UK, 2020–21	138
Table 11.3 UK	Summary of the gross incomes at the breakeven points in Table 11.2 UK	140
Table 11.4 UK	Gradual implementation of proposed alternative poverty benchmark BI	142
Table 11.2 Scot	Tax schedules, Scotland, 2020–21	142
Table 11.3 Scot	Summary of the gross incomes at the breakeven points in Table 11.2 Scot	144
Table 11.4 Scot	Gradual implementation of proposed alternative poverty benchmark BI	145
Table A.1	Figures for the UK, 2017–19	184
Table A.2	Figures for Scotland, 2017–19	187
Table B.1 Scot	Costing a BI model in £m for Scotland, 2020–21	188
Table B.1 UK	Costing a BI model in £m for the UK 2020–21	189
Table B.2 Scot	A method for costing a BI model for Scotland, 2020–21	190
Table B.2 UK	A method for costing a BI model for the UK, 2020–21	191
Table B.3	BIs by household type	192
Table C	Excel template for designing and costing your own preferred BI model for the UK	194

List of Abbreviations

AIDS	Acquired immune deficiency syndrome
AHC	After Housing Costs have been deducted
BHC	Before Housing Costs have been deducted
BI	Basic Income
BIEN	Basic Income European/Earth Network
Blue Book	UK National Accounts, published each year
BSP	Basic state pension
CB	Child Benefit
CBINS	Citizen's Basic Income Network Scotland
CBIT	Citizen's Basic Income Trust
CTB/CTR/CTS	Council Tax Benefit/Reduction/Support
CTC	Child Tax Credit
DB	Disability Benefit
DWP	Department for Work and Pensions
ESA	Employment and Support Allowance
GDP	Gross domestic product
HB	Housing Benefit
HBAI	Households Below Average Income
HES	Household economies of scale
HH	Household
HIV	Human immunodeficiency virus (infection)
HMRC	Her Majesty's Revenue and Customs
IS	Income Support
JSA	Jobseeker's Allowance
LP	Lone parent
LSE	London School of Economics
MDR	Marginal deduction rate
MIS	Minimum Income Standards
MP	Member of Parliament (Westminster)
MSP	Member of the Scottish Parliament

MTB	Means-tested benefit
NGO	Non-Governmental Organisation
NHS	National Health Service
NI/NIC	National Insurance/National Insurance Contribution
NIT	Negative income tax
NMW/NLW	National Minimum Wage/National Living Wage
PA/PITA	Personal Allowance / Personal Income Tax Allowance
PAYE	Pay As You Earn
pens	pensioner
Pens Cred	Pension Credit
pre	pre-school child
prim	primary school child
PwC	Parent with care (primary care-giving parent)
S2P	State Second Pension
SA	Social Assistance
sec	secondary school child
SERPS	State Earnings Related Pension Scheme
SNAP	Scottish National Accounts Project
SRP	State Retirement Pension
STP	Single Tier Pension
TC	Tax credit
TUC	Trades Union Council
UBI	Unconditional or universal basic income
UC	Universal Credit
VAT	Value Added Tax
WWII	World War Two
Y-BAR	Mean gross income per head of man, woman and child

A note about terminology

A BASIC INCOME (BI) is defined as a periodic cash payment where the unit for delivery is the individual. It is universal for a defined population, is not means-tested, nor is the amount differentiated except by age, and it is unconditional. A full definition is given in chapter 3.

The concept has a fairly long history in the UK (see the Chronology in Appendix D), and during that time has had several different names, sometimes with extra conditions attached. In 1918, it was introduced as a 'state bonus'. The Social Credit Movement of the interwar period called it a 'national dividend'. Milton Friedman, an American Nobel Prize-winning economist, proposed the concept as a 'negative income tax' (NIT) in 1962, which, in its original incarnation, was based on the household. NIT in today's debates is often presented as a version of BI with an alternative method of administration, based on a fully integrated benefit and income tax system and paid in arrears. This is discussed further in chapter 9.

Another Nobel Prize-winning economist, James Meade, used the term 'social dividend' from 1935, but implied different things at different times – sometimes a needs-based system and sometimes as a payment to everyone with no differentiation. 'Social dividend' was the term commonly used until the early 1980s. Since then, the term used by the English-speaking world has been 'basic income', although in the USA it is often referred to as a 'basic income guarantee' (BIG). Some people dislike the term 'basic income', because they associate it with basic needs and it sounds too basic. But the term 'basic income' actually refers to the fact that it provides a base, foundation or floor on which people can build their lives. It is the basic source of income. The Basic Income Research Group (BIRG) was set up in 1984 and agreed to change its name to Citizen's Income Trust (CIT) in 1993 in order to comply with the conditions of a generous grant. It is the only organisation that has consistently used the term 'citizen's income' (CI), and this term is recognised in the UK. The late Professor Ailsa McKay of Glasgow Caledonian University, feminist economist and political activist, always referred to it as a 'citizen's basic income' (CBI). The founding group of the new Scottish charity, Citizen's Basic Income Network Scotland (CBINS), has adopted this term too, with its emphasis on citizenship. The terms CI, CBI and BI can be used interchangeably.

My own preferred term is 'basic income'. It is shorter, to the point, and avoids the problem of the apostrophe. The presence and position of the apostrophe is crucial, since it changes the meaning. The apostrophe before the 's' in 'citizen's income' emphasises that it must be paid on an individual basis.

The term 'unconditional basic income' was adopted for the European Citizens' Initiative (ECI on UBI) campaign in 2013. Since then, the abbreviation, UBI, has frequently been used, but has often been interpreted as 'universal basic income'. These terms are also interchangeable with 'basic income'. Both 'unconditional' and 'universal' are superfluous adjectives, since these are defining characteristics of a BI. A BI would not be a BI unless it is both universal and unconditional.

Not only has the concept been known by different names over time, but during the recent rising interest in basic income, people are using the term 'basic income' to refer to different concepts, leading to a confusing proliferation of systems all being referred to by the same name.

It would be useful to have a standard definition for a BI, to which everyone could refer, and I would like to suggest that the definition provided by the Basic Income Earth Network (BIEN) – the international BI organisation which 'aims to serve as a link between all individuals and groups interested in basic income' – should be the starting point. The commentary on the BIEN definition has involved five characteristics – periodic, cash, individual, universal and unconditional.

However, a confusion had arisen because the term 'unconditional' has been used in two senses. The most common usage refers to the absence of any behavioural requirements or obligations. The second use of the term 'unconditional' refers to the amount of the BI not varying on account of categories of recipients or their circumstances, except that it could be age-related.

Thus, the same term has been used for two very different characteristics of BI (Standing, 2017: 6), which should appear separately in the definition. Part of the problem has been that of finding a satisfactory name for the second characteristic. Both Van Parijs et al (2017: 8) and Standing use the term 'uniform', and the term 'equal' also comes to mind. I propose the adoption of the term 'uniform' for this new characteristic.

Any system that was not based on BIEN's six revised characteristics could not be a genuine basic income. For instance, a 'minimum income guarantee' (MIG) is similar to a BI, but it is both *targeted* on people with insufficient income and gives each of them *just enough* to raise them up to a given income threshold. Similarly, a system similar to basic income, but which is *conditional* on recipients participating in society via authorised activities is a 'participation income'. The questions then arise of a) who decides what will be the approved types of participation; b) what will be the cost, both in terms of the bureaucracy to monitor the system, and the intrusion into people's lives; and c) what happens to those who are non-compliant? A BI is paid unconditionally to everyone, rich and poor.

Some proposed schemes may be based on the BIEN definition, and *augment* it, but these augmentations should be made clear.

In *A Basic Income Handbook*, I chose the term 'selectivity' to refer to *differentiation*, that is, the practice of paying different amounts of a benefit to different people. However, this was totally incorrect. Spicker reviewed the use of 'selectivity' within the public policy literature, where it means 'a process in which people are identified and selected to receive benefits', that is, a type of *eligibility* process based on exclusion (2005: 349). I apologise for any confusion caused. In order to avoid further confusion, I have dropped the term 'non-selectivity'.

In the UK, the welfare state comprises the public welfare services together with the cash-based, income maintenance Social Security system, which itself is divided into the contributory National Insurance system and the (mainly means-tested) Social Assistance safety net. In some countries, the term 'social security' refers exclusively to their contributory national insurance system.

Preface

I WAS DELIGHTED when Luath Press invited me to write a shorter, less academic version of my book, *A Basic Income Handbook*, published in 2017. But this is not just a summarised version of the original. So, what is different?

I am aware that I am not alone in having difficulty in creating a satisfactory structure into which to place theory and evidence about BI. Despite the concept of a BI being fairly simple, the subject matter (BI as the instrument – the 'how' – and the policy objectives – the 'why') is complex and inter-related. Also, a BI system has such a fundamentally different *raison d'être* compared with a typical social security system, that its effects would ramify throughout society, and its design and implementation would quickly become complex and technical. This leads to some repetition in the text.

So, do we start with the current problems, their historical development, or with the broader schools of philosophy and political ideologies into which BI fits? Or we could start directly with examining the idea of a basic income. I have chosen to start with a vision of the different society that I would like to help to create for myself and for future generations, while acknowledging that some people are happy with our current society, which suits them very well, and, of course, they are entitled to demur.

A section identifying the failures of the UK National Insurance system and the structural faults in the Social Assistance safety net has been developed further and more systematically in chapter 2.

Chapter 3 brings together the defining characteristics of the generic BI and their anticipated outcomes, and identifies the means by which the former help to bring about the latter.

My focus on the definition of the generic BI is accompanied by an appeal to those in educational or advisory roles to use technical terms accurately – income, finance, money and cash are not necessarily interchangeable, for instance. Welfare state, public welfare services, social security, national insurance and social assistance comprise another set of terms that should be used correctly. This helps to educate the public, many of whom are not familiar with their correct usage. Not doing so also risks being completely misunderstood. Those who do know what these terms mean will assume that the speaker or writer does also, and if she claims that a BI will replace the 'welfare state', when she should have referred to the 'social security system', it will be assumed that she wishes to do away with all the current public welfare services.

Although basic income has tended to be associated with the left, it also has its advocates on the right, which has raised concerns in some as to how it can be adopted by both ends of the political spectrum. However, basic income is not just about a single policy objective, such as alleviating poverty, but can help to fulfil a portfolio of aims – equity, community, choice and efficiency – which appeals legitimately to both left and right, but with different priorities attached to the various goals.

BIs have been taken up enthusiastically by right-wing free-market billionaires, especially in North America, wanting to accompany it with the ending of all public welfare services. However, we who value our public welfare services in the UK must reclaim our democracy, and campaign actively for both our welfare services and a generous BI. A BI system can lay the foundation for a good society and economy, but it is not a panacea for all ills, and needs to be supported by a range of services, and, indeed, by their further enhancement.

PART II offers descriptions of some BI schemes and pilot experiments carried out in the last half century, initially in North America, then in developing countries and more recently in Europe.

The characteristics of the generic BI define a class of income maintenance systems, within which a wide variety of models or schemes is possible. Part III explores the process of designing and costing BI models in a systematic way, presenting separate examples for the UK, and for Scotland as a fiscally-devolved nation.

In *A Basic Income Handbook*, I implied that a partial BI may be sufficient for working age adults, but now I am aware that this could compromise many people who are not registered as disabled, but who nonetheless would not necessarily be able to earn enough to top up their partial BIs from earnings. I now very much favour a model with a full BI income for *all* adults (which I define as 0.40 of mean gross income per head of man, woman and child), and a relatively generous child BI (0.20 of mean gross income per head) for those BI systems which do not include an element to cover housing costs. I also favour a small Personal Income Tax Allowance.

I still favour financing BI models via a *progressive* restructured income tax system in which the many tax loopholes, by which wealthier taxpayers are able to avoid paying their fair share of taxes, will be closed. However, it is impossible to estimate the cost of financing the BI scheme by a progressive income tax schedule without access to data on the distribution of gross incomes of *all* individuals, which is not available in the UK. Thus, I estimate the cost of financing each scheme, using a *proportionate* income tax (straight-line tax, or flat tax), which provides a useful, single summary figure by which to compare the costs of different models. This type of model turns out to be so efficient that it would be almost impossible to prevent wealthier individuals from profiting from the introduction of even a generous BI scheme as described above, without the introduction of higher income tax rates on higher incomes to create a breakeven point.

I am indebted to Noguera (2018) for his thought-provoking presentation, in which he drew attention to the confusion invoked by my inadequate definition of the *sum of net transfers* (Miller, 2017: 149), and which has helped me, I hope, to clarify the situation in chapter 10.

In addition to updating all the data necessary for devising BI models for the fiscal year 2020–21, using the same sources, assumptions and methods as in *A Basic Income Handbook*, I address several practical problems in chapters 10 and 11:

- How to avoid the parallel income tax schedules which can result when adults of different ages receive different levels of BI.
- How to calculate the extra cost in terms of lost tax revenue due to the creation of a small Personal Allowance at the lower end of the income distribution in the BI model.
- A simple method for estimating an approximate figure for the tax rate required to finance a BI model with only two different levels – one for adults, the other for dependent children.
- How to calculate the gross income at which the breakeven point would occur, for a BI model financed by income tax compared with the current income tax schedules.

I am in favour of gradual implementation over a short period, to avoid any potential disruption that such a radical change could induce if implemented all at once. Gradual implementation would involve the closing of tax loopholes and the gradual increase in tax rates by stages, say, every two years, over a planned, limited period. This would allow the minority who pay slightly more in taxes each time to realise that it is not a terrible disaster, but something that they can easily accommodate, and celebrate the emancipatory effects on the rest of society that their tax contributions will have made.

PART IV starts with a systematic exploration of the effects of a BI on the economy in chapter 12. It is followed by a new chapter comparing computer-based tax-benefit micro-simulation models with BI pilot experiments, and exploring the anatomy of the latter, describing the process and some of the issues involved. It becomes obvious that BI pilots are lengthy and expensive undertakings and their results are unlikely to be available for some years. Chapter 14 examines some of the objections to BI and concludes with some aspects of the political process with respect to implementation.

As in the *Handbook*, Appendix A provides a table of relevant data for the UK and Scotland that could be useful for those who wish to develop their own BI models. The 'work book' in Appendix B enables readers to design and cost them.

A new section has drawn together the objections to, criticisms of, and scepticism about BI, together with their counter-arguments, in Appendix E, as *'Aye, but...'*

Finally, I would like to share the fact that I am dyslexic (with a touch of dyspraxia), because this may give confidence to others who share this condition. All dyslexics manifest with different symptoms. Mine is based on a short-term memory problem. I was fortunate enough that the methods taught when I was in school gave me some coping strategies, but my reading speed has always been painfully slow. I was ashamed of this and the resultant narrowness of my acquaintance with literature and did my best to hide it. The advent of personal computing opened up a whole new world. Word processing surely must have been made with dyslexics in mind. At last, one can use a spell-check, and rewrite and edit papers to one's heart's content. Even with coping strategies and a word processor, I am still slow at everything that I do. Also, my short-term memory problem means that I have to discern whether any current reading will be important enough in the future to commit it to my long-term memory, which is very tiring. My condition was not diagnosed until my early fifties. With many disabilities, there is often a compensation. Dyslexics have two such gifts. We are recognised as being very creative, and many of us excel in art colleges and engineering faculties. We are also very intuitive and some use this in complementary therapy work. I encourage my fellow dyslexics to embrace their condition, to learn coping strategies, and to develop and celebrate their wonderful gifts. We are in exalted company.

The UK General Election in December 2019 delayed the usual Autumn Budget until 11 March 2020. All the tables and data in this book have been updated with the information available at that date, as though for a typical fiscal year in 2020–21.

However, events have been overtaken by the onslaught of COVID-19. No attempt has been made here to keep up with the rapid flow of policies from the UK government trying to reduce its ravages to health, incomes and the macro-economy.

There could be no stronger case than this pandemic for the immediate implementation of a full basic income in the UK, and across the world, which would have provided for basic needs and given financial security, reducing fear and anxiety. It could also have reduced the effect of the pandemic on the macro-economy by ensuring that sufficient spending power, and thus the supply of goods and services to satisfy needs, were protected.

Acknowledgements

As always, I am enormously indebted to my fellow trustees of both CBIT and CBINS, from whom I continue to learn so much. This book is a shorter version of *A Basic Income Handbook*, published in 2017, so all the acknowledgements and thanks for help with that book are also extended here. During the autumn of 2018, I enjoyed discussions and correspondence with Professor Paul Spicker, whom I would describe as a friendly critic of BI, and these have helped me to improve the accuracy of my knowledge about the current Social Security system in the UK. In addition, I thank Anne Gray, Greg Michaelson, Paul Spicker and Thomas Torrance for reading the typescript and for helpful comments. I thank Jim Pym for his help with copy-editing and proof-reading. I also thank Tom Sommerville for the cover photo. Any errors in this book are my responsibility alone.

PART I

Means and Ends

A basic income is a periodic cash payment unconditionally delivered to all on an individual basis, without means test or work requirement.

BASIC INCOME EARTH NETWORK (BIEN)

CHAPTER 1

Values and Vision

Imagine...

IMAGINE A SOCIETY where every adult receives a regular, unconditional, cash payment on an individual basis that is delivered automatically to one's personal account. This basic income (BI) is enough to live on modestly, but with dignity, enabling one to participate in public life. There is no compulsion to work, but most people want to work-for-pay to top up their incomes, to meet other people, for job satisfaction and to be recognised as someone who contributes to society. Some want to work long hours on a high salary; others prefer part-time work which fits in better with their work-life balance. Others take time out of paid work in order to care for children and elders, or other family members and friends with disabilities. Although automation has replaced many jobs, there is still demand for highly qualified workers in the new industries, in addition to demand for paid carers, those in the personal services and the creative arts.

Taxes on scarce resources ensure that it is non-material economic activity that continues to grow. There is a buzz in society as many people use their creative abilities to design new products, to make things, and invent new processes. Education is a growth sector, not just for training people to work, but because learning can be enjoyable and satisfying for its own sake. Leisure is another growth industry. Many take up hobbies such as handcrafts, gardening and rambling. The arts in many forms take off, for both participant and spectator. Increased financial security has led to a reduction in both incidence and depth of poverty. The fear, stress and anxiety have lifted and there is a general improvement in health. There is also a reduction in crime. Although one is not protected against the ordinary sorrows in life, optimism is in the air, accompanied by a palpable feeling of goodwill to and from those around them. People co-operate on local ventures.

Some societies appear to operate on the basis of fear and despair. BI provides a basis of compassion, justice, trust and hope. Let us work together to turn this dream into reality.

Thus opened the introduction to *A Basic Income Handbook*. It is a vision worth repeating.

What sort of society do we wish to create for ourselves and for future generations?

When proposing a particular reform, it is also important to give one's vision of society, to assess whether that reform represents a move in the right direction. It is often claimed that the first duty of government should be the security of its people. This ought to mean their *income security*. Or, more explicitly, it is the first duty of government to provide the means for all individuals to meet their basic needs for a dignified, if modest, standard of living, enabling them to participate in cultural, social and public life, and to develop and flourish to their full potential in a sustainable economy as a human right. One might hope that this would help to create a society very different from the self-preoccupied, materialistic and cruel one that the UK has become.

Engraved on the Scottish Mace at Holyrood are the words: 'wisdom, justice, compassion, integrity'. These are the ideals to which the people in Scotland aspire for their Members of the Scottish Parliament (MSPs). These values would provide a good foundation for a replacement income maintenance system in the form of a basic income (BI). They could transform our society, from the present one of fear and despair, to the alternative described above, based on compassion, justice, trust and hope.

A BI comprises a set of instruments rather than a program of policy objectives; that is, it is a means to several ends, depending on the other instruments with which the BI is coupled. The ends indicate the 'why', and the means provide the 'how'. The ends to which it could lead include freedom, fairness and fellowship (expressing the familiar concepts of *liberté*, *egalité*, and *fraternité* in a different way), which are outcomes that many people in our society would like to enjoy.

A BI system would be a reform of, or replacement for, much of the current Social Security system only. BIs are not, cannot be, nor should be claimed as, a replacement for the *whole* of the welfare state. A BI is a necessary condition for a better society, but it would have to be supported by many other public welfare services. These include health and social care, childcare provision, services for people with disabilities, personal social services, social housing, education for life and for skills-training, public transport, in addition to policies to redistribute wealth, and to invest in infrastructure. Sadly, welfare services have been undermined by recent UK governments, with tragic consequences for the most vulnerable.

A BI system, designed for the 21st century, is a radical alternative to much of the current Social Security system, leading to new relationships between society, the state and its citizens.

Justification for a BI system

> Everyone has the right to a standard of living adequate for the health and well-being of himself and of his family, including food, clothing, housing and medical care and necessary social services, and the right to security in the event of unemployment, sickness, disability, widowhood, old age or other lack of livelihood in circumstances beyond his control – Universal Declaration of Human Rights, Article 25 (1).

This was adopted by the General Assembly of the United Nations on 10 December 1945. This right is granted (by implication) only to the head of the household and only *in circumstances beyond a person's control*. Thus, while it is on the right path, it only takes us part way towards a BI, which is granted without those qualifications.

Thomas Paine (1796) argued that the land and natural resources belong to the people. Since land has been appropriated for private use, the owners owe a rent to the whole excluded population.

Our economy is built on the infrastructure and material heritage of previous generations. Part of the BI can be regarded as a dividend from the economy, which is underpinned by this common heritage.

'A 2005 World Bank study concluded that most of a nation's wealth derives from intangible capital; that is, from human capital and the quality of institutions, especially the rule of law. The wealthier the nation, the more this is so.' Thus, we all help to create our society and are shareholders in its wealth. Part of the BI can be regarded as a further dividend from this common good.

In 1624, John Donne declared 'No man is an island'. In other words, we all are dependent on many others. Our decisions and actions affect other people. We are interdependent and therefore mutually responsible for each other.

Recent estimates indicate that one fifth of the population in the UK lives below the poverty line, including one fifth of the children, which affects their life chances. Evelyn Forget (2018) described how poverty affects health. Poverty is not just a matter of material deprivation. It also includes both the external effect of stigma and its internalisation by the victim, lowering her self-esteem. It involves insecurity both from the precarious nature of much employment, and from the uncertainties associated with the Social Security system, leading to chronic stress. It is also affected by the loss of social solidarity resulting from the exclusion and rejection associated with an unequal and divided society, which undermines mental health. Poverty shortens life by as much as 12 years between the life expectancy of those in the bottom 10 per cent and the top 10 per cent of the UK income distribution.

Even prisoners receive three meals a day, so why not people whose only crime is that of being poor? Within six months of having their disability benefits withdrawn, 1,600 disabled people committed suicide. In England and Wales, 726 homeless people died prematurely in 2018, with an average age of 45 for men, and 43 for women. On average, two rough sleepers die on the streets each week in the UK.

The right to life is a matter of ethics and should take precedence over financial considerations.

The most compelling justification for a BI is that the current Social Security system in the UK is complex, unjust, unwieldy, inefficient and not fit for purpose. It fails to protect many of the most vulnerable people in our society. It was designed for the very different economy and society of seven decades ago and is now well past its sell-by date.

The case for vertical redistribution of income from rich to poor

It is claimed in chapter 3 that a BI could help to redistribute income from rich to poor, and, in chapter 10, that this could be brought about more effectively if accompanied by a progressive income tax system. Horizontal redistribution is usually acceptable, that is, having received support during childhood, one is taxed during the main working part of one's life, in order to receive a pension later. However, there are some compelling reasons for vertical redistribution:

- To counteract the tendency of markets to redistribute from poor to rich. Not even neoclassical economists have put forward a theorem, let alone evidence, to demonstrate that the 'perfect competition market' will redistribute from rich to poor; it merely keeps the *status quo* at best. Neither has any evidence been provided in support of the trickle-down 'theory' as an effective mechanism of redistribution.

- To reverse the current tide of increasing inequality since 1979 (evidenced by the increased Gini coefficient – a measure of inequality), which successive governments have failed to stem, or have even encouraged.

- The wealth of our current society is the result of the accumulation of ideas, labour and capital of earlier generations, and who is to say whose forebears they were? Everyone should be able to benefit from it.

- No one can claim to be self-made unless they have lived alone on a deserted island from birth. Since this is impossible, everyone will have benefitted from society.

- Those with secure, well-paid employment have a responsibility to those without.

- Many poor people work hard, too, and yet are unable to earn their way out of poverty. The majority of children in poverty in the UK live in households where one or both parents are in work.
- Support for families with dependent children is essential, and not just because children will become the providers of society's pensions and care in old age, both for those who have raised them and for others of their generation.
- More equal societies have been better for everyone, even the better off, as evidenced in Wilkinson and Pickett's *The Spirit Level* (2009).
- The best democracy is one with a more equal income distribution.

Who are the rich?

For many of us, a rich person is someone who appears to have greater income or wealth than ourselves. It is a loose term and could apply to many different circumstances.

If the UK mid-year 2018 population of nearly 66.5 million individuals were divided into poor and rich halves, then every income taxpayer would belong to the rich half. Some 31.0 million people were forecast to have paid income tax in 2018–19, of whom 6.37 million were aged 65 or over. Another 17 million working age adults (aged 16–64) had too small an income on which to pay tax. Among the taxpayers, 4.28 million paid the higher rate of income tax and 0.393 million were liable for the additional rate. If referring only to the *adult* population of 53.8 million, then about 4.1 million lower-income taxpayers would appear in the poorer half.

The mean gross income per head of man, woman and child in 2018 was £24,595 for the UK, and £21,068 in Scotland.

A very simplistic division between poor and rich could be between those who have less and those who have more than the mean. Since the distribution of gross income is very unequal, there are far more people whose income is below the mean than with income above it.

One could define 'the rich', 'the richer' and 'the richest' as the top 10 per cent, 1 per cent and the 0.1 per cent in the country respectively, by income and assets. In the UK in 2018, the mid-year population was just over 66 million people, so these represent the richest 6.6 million, 0.66 million and 66,000 people in the country respectively. It can be difficult to identify who these people are. However, *The Sunday Times* publishes its Rich List of the 1,000 'super-rich' people living and working in the UK.

It is anticipated that redistribution of income from rich to poor would mean that the top 20–30 per cent of individuals in the gross income distribution would experience a fall in their net incomes. The actual loss would depend on several factors, such as the level of their gross income, the actual BI model, and how it was financed. This is explored further in chapters 10 and 11. A wealthy individual may suffer a fall in net income, but other members of his/her family may experience gains, so that the household may not necessarily be worse off financially.

CHAPTER 2

What is wrong with the current UK Social Security system?

The National Insurance (NI) system

BEVERIDGE'S *Report on Social Insurance and Allied Services* of 1942 was a bestseller. He identified five giant evils in society: want, ignorance, squalor, idleness and disease. The solutions implemented by the Attlee government immediately after WWII were a Social Security system, the 1944 Education Act, an extensive house-building program, full employment policy and the NHS respectively. Together they form the basis of the welfare state. Thus, the welfare state comprises the public welfare services together with the cash-based, income maintenance Social Security system, which itself is divided into the contributory National Insurance system and the (mainly means-tested) Social Assistance safety net. Beveridge's report led directly to the National Insurance Act of 1946 and the National Assistance Act of 1948 – designed for a society and an economy that were very different from those of today.

The NI system was designed around men's employment patterns of the post WWII period, and has never met women's needs, unless they were competing in the workplace on men's terms. The NI benefits were intended to be *income-replacements* for the main earner at times of sickness, unemployment and retirement. The National Assistance, or Social Assistance (SA), system was intended to be a (mainly means-tested) safety net, with less generous benefits. The NI benefits in the UK have become eroded over time and are no longer sufficient to meet a person's needs – and were sometimes less than the means-tested benefit (MTB) levels, which themselves have been eroded.

The amounts of the NI benefits are based on an individual's contribution record: gaps lead to reduced benefits. Many of the NI benefits are also time-limited, usually for six months (but, obviously, not for the State Retirement Pension). The criteria for unemployment benefits have introduced rigidities into the system that discourage part-time work. However, some people fall through bigger gaps, by not being able to build up a contribution record at all. Many women, while caring for children, elders and others, still fall into this category. Nor is the NI system really designed for self-employed people, who do not enjoy the same protection as employees.

An NI system requires that nearly everyone is in paid employment. According to *The Blue Book* (2019, T 1.5), in the UK in 2018, there were 4.780 million self-employed workers and 27.494 million employees, with 1.380 million unemployed people, giving a total of 33.819 million adults who were 'economically active'. The other 19.215 million adults are labelled as 'economically inactive'. Even excluding 12.166 million aged 65 or over, it still leaves at least 7.049 million people of *working age* who were 'economically inactive'. Thus, nearly 17 per cent of the working age population (total 41.6 million, aged 16–64, in 2018) were economically inactive. About 2.5 million of these would have been people with disabilities, many of whom are unable to work. Another 5 million working age adults acted as unpaid care-givers, some of whom will have received the princely sum of £67.25 per week as Carer's Allowance in 2020–21, if they cared for someone with a disability for at least 35 hours each week (less than £2 per hour).

Those who gain most from the NI system are those in well-paid, full-time, secure employment over a lifetime. It does not necessarily serve others very well. The labour market has changed dramatically over the last seven decades, and now many people have a portfolio of low-skilled, low-waged, part-time, short-term, insecure, joyless jobs in the gig economy. The NI system does not cover the whole population and it fails some of the most vulnerable people in society.

Structural faults in the Social Assistance system

Some of those who are not eligible for NI benefits can apply for means-tested and other benefits via the SA 'safety net'. However, the NI and SA benefits are well below poverty level, being about half the level recommended by the EU's official poverty benchmark (incorporated into UK legislation in the Child Poverty Act 2010–16, and discussed further in chapter 8). In addition, the SA system suffers from some major structural faults.

UK marriage law is a relic from Medieval times, when a wife was one of her husband's chattels (a property item). Owners have economic rights but their chattels do not. This model of marriage is imprinted on the whole of the UK Social Security system and is extended to all cohabiting couples (married, in a civil partnership, or otherwise cohabiting). This helps to explain why *the primary unit for assessment and delivery of SA is the couple*, so that a couple must make a joint application.

Rather than being a contract between the partners, marriage in the UK is a contract between the state and the couple. The spouses agree to aliment (maintain) each other in a style appropriate to the standard of living of the wealthier partner. This ensures that the poorer partner is not a burden on the state. A main earner receives an 'income-replacement' NI benefit with additions for his dependents. It is only when he cannot maintain himself (and his chattels), and the couple as a unit becomes in need, that it can apply jointly for SA benefits.

Thus, the poorer partner is denied access to benefits on her own account. She may have no independent income of her own (except perhaps Child Benefit) with which to feed herself and her children. Nor is she legally entitled to any of her partner's income. This out-dated law traps the poorer partner, usually the female, into the humiliating role of financial dependent, which should be an anachronism in the 21st century. While the current marriage law is gender neutral, it is gendered in its effect, affecting many women adversely. Most other non-cohabiting adults who share accommodation are assessed as individuals.

Eligibility for access to the SA system is *targeted* on particular groups in society, usually based on categories of people or their circumstances. Administrative problems can arise when the categories are not discrete, or the circumstances change frequently. The SA system in the UK is targeted on poorer people. Rather than protecting them, as claimed, targeting segregates them, making it easier to identify and stigmatise, humiliate and reject them. Many claimants report that the rejection by society is even more painful than trying to survive on below-poverty level benefits. It leads to a low take-up of the benefits to which poor people are entitled. In contrast, systems that give universal access, such as the NHS, are popular with all and thus protect the poorest, and often are cheaper to run.

The *means-testing of benefits* increases the rate at which deductions are made from earnings, effectively decreasing net wage rates, and introducing an inherent disincentive to work-for-pay that cannot be avoided. When unemployed and low-paid workers in the UK try to earn their way out of poverty, they not only face the deduction of income tax and NI contributions, but the withdrawal rates of their means-tested benefits are aggregated and also deducted from their earnings. Some claimants in the UK can face punitive marginal deduction rates of nearly 96 per cent. This creates a regressive system, where claimants face far higher effective tax rates than are levied on those on the highest incomes (of over £150,000 pa), whose income tax rate is 45 per cent and NI contribution is 2 per cent. The means-testing of benefits is the result of a combination of targeting on poor people, and differentiation, where the amounts of the MTBs vary according to the means (income) of the claimant. Sometimes savings are taken into account too, which discourages saving, and reduces poor people's resilience in times of hardship.

The means-testing of in-work benefits rewards employers, since the loss in wages will be partially compensated for by the increased MTBs. This gives employers an incentive to reduce wage rates.

SA benefits are *differentiated*; that is, different levels of entitlement are granted to people who are otherwise equally eligible. Variations in the level of payment could be smooth, calculated using a withdrawal taper, or in steps, using thresholds. Eligibility and differentiation can be based on similar categories and circumstances. Differentiation could be based on some personal attribute that one cannot change (such as chronological age or ethnic origin), or on household relationships, status or living arrangements. In the UK, notions of worth or desert used to lead to differential entitlement, such that 'deserving' widows received more generous benefits than 'undeserving' unmarried mothers. Despite – or maybe because of – the humiliation of all those claimants receiving SAs, by some sections of the media, this particular distinction is less obvious today.

In the UK, cohabiting couples are granted less in benefits than two singletons, to prevent the partners from receiving more than they 'need'. If partners struggling with poverty realise that they could be better off financially if they lived apart, then this type of differentiation can be seen as the potential cause of the break-up of families. Again, this is the result of the UK's medieval marriage laws. It is also both intrusive and unjust.

SA benefits are *conditional*. In order to receive their MTBs, claimants usually have to fulfil conditions designed to change their behaviour. It is still the case that some claimants are forced to behave according to traditional gender roles, such as with the intrusive and distasteful 'cohabitation rule'. A single female or lone mother receiving an enhanced benefit compared with a co-habiting woman could lose her benefits if a man were observed spending more than three nights each week with her on a regular basis, on the assumption that he is a traditional male breadwinner financially supporting the dependent female home-maker.

Formerly, claimants had to prove that they were 'available for work'. Now the conditionality is much harsher, and claimants must 'prove that they have been actively seeking work for 35 hours each week', which, for a measly £74.35 per week, represents a rate of compensation of just over £2 per hour, well below the National Living Wage. Failure to achieve this target can lead to crippling sanctions, such as losing two weeks-worth of benefits, both for themselves and their children, forcing them into deep indebtedness or risking destitution. Poverty adversely affects a child's lifetime prospects.

These same sanctions can be applied to even minor misdemeanours, such as being late for an appointment at the

Jobcentre office, even for reasons outwith the claimant's control (such as her child-minding arrangements falling through at the last minute, or being at a parent's funeral, being at a job interview, or even for working). This creates chronic stress and anxiety that undermines health, making extra demands on the NHS. Conditionality and sanctions require extra monitoring and administration compared with a system without conditions, leading to increased intrusion, risk of error and fraud, and to increased administration costs.

The current means-tested benefit system in the UK is not only misogynistic, divisive and stigmatising, oppressive and punitive, but it also discourages people from working for pay.

Would an improved NI and SA system be achievable in the UK?

Some hard-working, well-paid (mainly) men of a certain age claim that an improved NI system would meet the Social Security needs of the UK. However, even if the UK's NI system could be improved (for instance, in the ways recommended by Spicker, 2017), including more generous benefit levels, less harsh conditionality and sanctions, and notwithstanding the other structural flaws in the MTB system, are the necessary conditions likely to prevail in the UK?

The Nordic countries have a variety of social security systems based on NI, which have worked well for them. They have well-educated populations, with full employment, high wage rates, state-funded childcare provision with highly-qualified nursery staff, and generous NI benefits financed by high taxation rates. Usually both parents work, not just because of the health and social advantages, but because of the high cost of living. The Nordic countries have a good work culture. However, cracks have begun to appear in their systems, on account of increased unemployment.

The UK tends to educate the more academically able half of its population. Some pupils are still illiterate when they leave school. Many more leave with poor work skills to sell on the labour market. It could take a generation to repair this neglect. In addition, the costs of childcare services in the UK are some of the highest in Europe

Despite government claims of near full employment in the UK, this includes the 'full employment' of people in low-waged, part-time, short-term, insecure employment, which keeps them in poverty (rather than well-paid, full-time, secure jobs for all). For many, it is a work culture of 'nose to the grindstone of work-for-pay in joyless jobs'. The system drives the most vulnerable people to take any job available in order to reduce expenditure on the Social Security system, and to increase economic growth, which in turn tends to benefit the top 40 per cent of the UK income distribution.

An NI system requires that most people work-for-pay and make NI contributions out of their earnings to build up a contribution record. Yet, as estimated above, nearly 17 per cent of the working age population in the UK were 'economically inactive' in 2018.

The current Social Security system in the UK is broken. If we were to design a Social Security system from scratch today, we would be unlikely to end up with the current National Insurance and Social Assistance 'safety net' systems. It is a Gordian knot that cannot be unravelled or reformed. It needs to be cut through and replaced by a radical alternative, designed for the 21st century. That alternative should be a BI. It represents a new relationship between society, the state and its citizens. A BI system could work well in either the current labour market situation or an economy affected by a further loss of jobs as a result of automation.

While increasing the NI and SA benefit levels for those who are eligible would be welcome, in order to meet the official poverty benchmark, it would not by itself solve the problems identified in this chapter. Fortunately, when the structural flaws in the current SA system have been addressed and corrected, a BI system emerges.

CHAPTER 3
The generic basic income

What is a basic income?

IN 'A NOTE ABOUT TERMINOLOGY', some of the different English language names were listed that the concept of a basic income has been given over the last century, and conversely, many different proposals that have been labelled as a 'basic income' recently were noted.

I suggested that there should be a standard definition for a basic income, to which everyone could refer. That standard should be provided by the international organisation, Basic Income Earth Network (BIEN). However, the commentary on the definition, describing its characteristics, is undergoing one of its occasional revisions, both to rectify an omission and to clarify the definition in order to be able distinguish a BI from related concepts.

The omission has arisen because the term 'unconditional' is often used to refer to two very different meanings which should be distinguished from each other, and both included in the definition. When most advocates and critics of BI use the term 'unconditional', they mean 'free of behavioural requirements', or 'obligation-free'. This contrasts with the new characteristic, where the amount of the BI does not vary according to categories or circumstances (except that it could be age-related), and which the term 'uniform' describes more accurately.

BIEN's constitutional definition and proposed commentary could now read as follows:

A **basic income** is a periodic cash payment unconditionally delivered to all on an individual basis, without means test or work requirement.

That is, basic income has *six* **characteristics**: it is periodic, a cash payment, individual-based, universal, uniform (except by age) and unconditional.

These six characteristics are defined as follows:

1 **Periodic**: it is paid at the beginning of the period to which it relates, at regular intervals (for example every month), not as a one-off grant.

2 **Cash payment**: it is paid in an appropriate medium of exchange, allowing those who receive it to decide what they spend it on. It is not, therefore, paid either in kind (such as food or services) or in vouchers dedicated to a specific use. It is paid gross, that is, without any personal tax or other deductions.

3 **Individual**: it is delivered on an individual basis – and not, for instance, on the basis of a couple or household.

4 **Universal**: this indicates **who** is eligible, it is paid to all, including to a child to be administered on her/his behalf by the primary care-giving parent or another registered responsible person. It is not targeted at a particular section of the population according to specific categories or circumstances, such as an occupation group or low-income people.

5 **Uniform**: the **amount** of the basic income is **the same/ equal** for everyone within a given territorially-defined jurisdiction at a given time, except that it could vary by age, but not according to specific categories or circumstances, such as personal attributes, household living arrangements, employment status, insurance contribution record, income, wealth or worth.

6   **Unconditional**: a basic income is not conditional on the recipient having to fulfil any behavioural requirements, such as participating in authorised activities. It is paid without a requirement to work or to demonstrate willingness-to-work, to undertake volunteer work, or to behave according to traditional gender roles. In other words, it is **obligation-free**.

(BIEN: www.basicincome.org/basic-income/)

This definition precludes the means-testing of benefits which results from the combination of targeting people with low incomes, and reducing their payments as the gross income or wealth of the recipient increases, until the benefit has effectively been withdrawn.

BIEN's six characteristics, as proposed above, provide the standard definition for the generic basic income. Any system that does not fulfil these six characteristics cannot be claimed as a *genuine* basic income. General adoption of this definition of basic income could reduce confusion resulting from the use of the same term to apply to a plethora of different systems. Ignoring the 'universality' characteristic leads to a targeted income. Ignoring 'universality' and 'uniformity' could also give rise to a (means-tested) Minimum Income Guarantee, with a 100 per cent withdrawal rate on the lowest incomes. Ignoring the 'non-conditionality' criterion leads to a participation income. (Atkinson, 2015: 218–223).

Some proposed BI schemes could incorporate BIEN's characteristics but augment them, and the ways in which they differ from BIEN's should be clearly indicated. The six characteristics define a **class** of income maintenance systems, for which there is broad consensus. However, a wide range of BI **models or schemes** is possible within that class, and there is no consensus as to what their objectives should be. This is explored in chapter 8.

The BIEN website continues with:

> A wide variety of Basic Income proposals are circulating today. They differ along many other dimensions, including in the amounts of the Basic Income, the source of funding, the nature and size of reductions in other transfers that might accompany it, and so on.
>
> BIEN is a charitable organisation dedicated to taking an educational role, and therefore, it cannot endorse any particular proposal...
>
> A Basic Income that is stable in size and frequency and high enough to be, in combination with other social services, part of a policy strategy to eliminate material poverty and enable the social and cultural participation of every individual is often called a "full Basic Income", and a lower one is often called a "partial Basic Income". However, the definitions of "full" and "partial" are highly controversial, and BIEN has not attempted to define them officially.

The following sentence, which was omitted from this passage as a result of revision in 2016, should be re-instated in the paragraph above, before the last sentence:

> We oppose the replacement of social services or entitlements, if that replacement worsens the situation of relatively disadvantaged, vulnerable or lower-income people.

Obviously, it would help the poorest sections of society, if the BIs were to be delivered at the beginning of the period that they cover, providing a regular, predictable and reliable source of income. It is important that the level should be stable over time and protected from sudden declines. It also makes sense that the BI should be exempt from taxes on income, rather than paying out a larger BI that would then be subject to the tax.

Of course, if someone no longer met the eligibility criteria of her/his jurisdiction, s/he would no longer qualify to receive a BI. But, otherwise, the BI should be 'non-withdrawable'. No one should have their right to a BI withdrawn by the state except in the most extreme circumstances. Similarly, it should be made illegal for any private body or person to deprive an individual of their BI. For example, it should be made illegal to use a BI as security for a loan, even a mortgage, which, if things went wrong, (ending up with negative equity, for instance), could deprive the recipient of her/his future income stream and put them at risk of permanent destitution. A BI should be inalienable, protected from sequestration (debt-collection procedures), because it is a personal benefit.

What broad objectives could a basic income help to fulfil?

Each characteristic of a BI scheme could contribute to several related short-term and long-run objectives for welfare reform. A full basic income could lead to the following outcomes:

- Each person is respected and valued for her/his own sake. A BI bestows dignity, privacy and financial autonomy. By trusting adults with more control over the use of their time, together with financial security, a BI emancipates and empowers them, increasing their life choices. Emancipation is worth far more than the monetary value of the benefit.

- A BI can help to prevent, or at least reduce, income poverty, providing *financial security*, granting the right not to be destitute, and thus reducing anxiety and chronic stress. In the long run, it could increase well-being in terms of security, living standards, health and educational opportunities, helping people to develop to their full potentials, and reducing demands on health and other personal services.

- A BI could help to redistribute income, from rich to poor, men to women, and geographically. A flat rate would have a greater impact on those with no or low incomes than on those with high ones. It could heal our divided societies and eventually help to create a just, united and inclusive society. But *income* inequalities could be reduced most effectively, if the BI system were financed by a progressive *income tax* system.

- Non-means-testing of benefits restores the incentive to work-for-pay inherent in the wage rate. In the long run, it could lead to more efficient labour markets, giving more flexibility to employees, not just to employers, releasing creative enterprise and increasing productivity.

- A BI scheme can help to simplify the administration of a social security system, reducing the risk of fraud or error by either recipient or staff, and reducing both administration and compliance costs. It would be less intrusive into people's lives. It should also avoid the time-consuming personal effort and stress required of many claimants in order to apply for and retain means-tested benefits. Eventually it could lead to a more transparent and accountable administration system.

These five objectives can be summarised as: emancipation, well-being, an inclusive society, a more efficient, productive labour market and a simpler, less intrusive administration system. Obviously, BI is not about just a single-issue, and the combination of equity, community, choice and efficiency goals appeals to both left and right of the political spectrum.

How do the defining characteristics of a basic income help to fulfil the objectives?

The defining characteristics of the generic BI and the broad objectives to which they can contribute are inter-related. They do not consist of one-to-one relationships. The way in which each of the main characteristics (the instruments: individual basis, universality, non-differentiation and non-conditionality), influences each of the objectives (the outcomes: emancipation, well-being, inclusion, labour market flexibility, and a simpler administration system), is illustrated in Table 3.1.

All of the main characteristics are necessary to enable both men and women to experience emancipation and empowerment, financial security and well-being, a more just and united society, and good working relationships. The more generous the BI, the more that this would be so. Financial security is necessary for the full experience of the other outcomes.

Women comprise the largest single group of people who would benefit from a BI, particularly married women and those in civil partnerships or otherwise cohabiting, who would be released immediately from financial dependence that traps so many of them, and, with it, the threat of economic abuse. Having one's own unconditional source of income could emancipate and empower women, giving them more life choices. It would enable women to negotiate for a better allocation of domestic chores and caring responsibilities in the home. It gives them more control over

Table 3.1 How the defining characteristics of a

OBJECTIVES → CHARACTERISTICS that define a BI SYSTEM, below	Financial autonomy. Emancipation and empowerment of adults	Prevent income poverty; avoid stigma and provide financial security; lower stress increases well-being.
The unit for delivery is the **INDIVIDUAL**	Grants financial privacy and autonomy. Reduces inequality of power relationships in the home – fairer division of tasks.	Would give former 'financial dependents' the right to an income of their own for the first time – helps to liberate them from abusive partners.
Eligibility is UNIVERSAL (Avoids discrimination, targeting, division, stigma and low take-up).	Respects and values *all* individuals – a necessary condition for the emancipation and empowerment of *all* adults.	All adults eligible for an income for the first time. Helps to reduce the *incidence* of income poverty. Avoids stigma and low take-up. Protects the most vulnerable.
UNIFORM LEVELS OF BI, except that it could be age-related. (Avoids differentiation, stigma, division and low take-up – less intrusive.)	Avoids differentiation, stigma and division into 'deserving' and 'undeserving' poor. Helps to end the 'Cohabitation Rule'.	Avoids differentiation and stigma. Couples no longer discriminated against. Helps to end the 'Cohabitation Rule'. Restored incentives to work-for-pay help people to earn their way out of poverty.
UNCONDITIONAL No behavioural requirements re paid work, volunteering or gender roles. Less intrusive or demanding. Sanctions not necessary.	Respects and values all. Trusts adults with more control over the use of their own time. Increases life choices for all adults. Reduces inequality of power relationships in the household – enabling negotiations for fairer sharing of care and domestic tasks and of paid work.	Reduces *depth* of income poverty, and could prevent it, depending on the level of BI. Gives the unconditional right not to be destitute – provides financial security. Creates a safety net. Better work-life balance. Reduction of stress improves health and well-being – reducing cost to health and personal social services.
FINANCED BY A PROGRESSIVE INCOME TAX SYSTEM		The higher the income tax rates, the greater the BI, and the greater its impact on reduction of poverty.

basic income help to fulfil the broad objectives

Reduce income inequalities and divisions. Create a just, united and inclusive society.	Restore incentives to work. Labour market efficiency and flexibility; sustainable econ productivity and growth.	Simplify administration system, leading to greater transparency and accountability.
Liberates poorer partners from financial dependence. Redistribution within the household, and between rich and poor households.	Household economies of scale provide incentives for adults to share housing, and reduce demand for single person housing.	Simpler administration, less intrusive, but more tax / benefit units to assess.
Avoids discrimination, targeting, division and stigma. Universal systems are inclusive, popular and redistributive, and are often cheaper, specially for services.	Redistribution from rich to poor increases economic demand. Could help to regenerate areas of multiple deprivation.	More efficient (cheaper) to give BIs to all and to assess everyone once only each year via income tax. Could lead to even more tax units. Still monitoring for eligibility.
Avoids discrimination, stigma and division. Fosters social solidarity and community. Absence of benefit tapers makes the effective income tax system less regressive.	Reduces marginal deduction rates and restores incentives to work-for-pay for claimants, raising their net wage rates above their reservation wages. Wage rates adjust.	Differentiation reduced to a minimum. Less intrusive. Less reliance on MTBs simplifies social security administration, reducing risk of error and fraud, and reducing costs.
Inequality of income decreases as BI increases. Redistribution between paid and unpaid work. BI systems trust citizens to decide on their own contributions to society. Fosters community. Supports life-long learning and creative enterprise. Quality of life.	More training and work choice increases productivity. Financial security reduces inequality of power relationships in the workplace. Workers can negotiate for fair pay and better working conditions, depending on labour market situation – increases industrial democracy. Creative entrepreneurship.	Simplifies administration and compliance systems. Decouples income from paid work. No difference between in-work and out-of-work payments. Less intrusive. Avoids current time-consuming personal effort needed to apply for and retain benefits.
A more progressive income tax system could help to redistribute incomes more effectively.	Increased taxes on income could lead to an increase in hours worked by higher-waged workers.	A small Personal Allowance would avoid the need to submit a tax return merely for casual earnings.

major life choices, including leaving an abusive relationship or starting a new partnership, starting a family or having another child, moving to a larger house or downsizing, taking a job or starting a business.

However, the introduction of a BI scheme is also likely to affect men's lives. Many workers are aware that if they lost their jobs and were unable to find another one within two or three months, they would be at risk of losing their homes, marriages and families.

The guarantee of an income that could prevent destitution would also reduce anxiety levels and help to relieve other mental health problems. More men than now could have the option of choosing a more congenial work-life balance, and experience the joys and responsibilities of being involved in the daily care and upbringing of their children. Similarly, with a sufficiently generous BI, lone mothers and fathers and their children could live fuller lives.

Many people would like to help to care for close relatives and friends, especially ageing parents, but cannot afford to give up (even part of) their jobs in order to provide their services. A generous BI would give them the financial security to make that choice.

Young adults in late teenage years comprise another group who could benefit from a bit more independence, administering their own BIs and learning financial skills. They would continue to benefit as students, when their BIs could contribute towards their maintenance costs. Writers and other artists would value the security that a BI would give them while they are developing their creative talents and setting up their businesses. It could also enable people to update their work skills regularly, and help life-long education to become a reality. Others might prefer to use their BIs to take an occasional sabbatical to travel or achieve some artistic or other lifetime ambition.

It can be quite difficult to pick out other specific groups, because most people could be affected positively by the implementation of a BI scheme. But, as emphasised, the generosity of the scheme is crucial for providing financial security, which then provides the basis for real choice over the use of one's time and for true emancipation.

Table 3.2, 'The structure of income maintenance systems', summarises the main content of chapters 2 and 3. It uses the structure of income maintenance systems to compare the characteristics and outcomes of the typical means-tested benefit system (as described in chapter 2) with those of the generic BI definition. It lists some frequent criticisms of the generic BI definition, some of which are 'normative' (value-based) and others are 'positive' (and could be tested empirically). The last column of Table 3.2 offers some countervailing arguments to the criticisms. Note that Table 3.1 is an expansion of columns 4 and 5 of Table 3.2.

Table 3.2   The structure of typical income maintenance

INSTRUMENTS or FEATURES	CURRENT UK MTB SYSTEM	OUTCOME OF CURRENT UK SYSTEM	CHARACTERISTICS OF BI
UNIT for assessment and delivery of benefits.	The **COHABITING COUPLE** is the primary unit, then the individual.	An 'economically inactive' poorer partner has no right to an income of her/his own. Unequal power relationships in the home are damaging and demeaning.	The unit is the **INDIVIDUAL**.
ELIGIBILITY indicates *who* is included	**TARGETING** of benefits according to specific categories or circumstances, such as on particular income groups. Divisive.	Targeting benefits on poorest people does not protect them. Instead it segregates, stigmatises, humiliates and rejects them – very painful. Low take-up of the benefits to which they are entitled.	**UNIVERSAL** for a given population – how to define it and devise eligibility criteria? Avoids targeting, stigma and low take-up.
ENTITLEMENT CRITERIA indicate the *amounts* of benefits by category or circumstance of recipient.	**DIFFERENT AMOUNTS**, by *personal attributes, or *on frequently changing relationships and circumstances, or *means (gross income or wealth) of recipient, or *worth.	Stigmatising, divisive, intrusive and unjust. A couple receives less than two singletons; this also leads to the intrusive and distasteful 'Cohabitation Rule'. It increases admin costs and the risks of errors and fraud. Benefit tapers introduce inherent disincentives to work-for-pay and poverty traps, and are very regressive.	**UNIFORM levels**, except that it could be age-related. The level of the BI does not vary according to categories or circumstances such as household living arrangements, employment status, means or worth.
CONTINGENCY – via *behavioural* requirements	Harsh **PRE-CONDITIONS** imposed. Eg. formerly in UK 'availability for work; now 'give evidence for 35 hours per week of active search for paid work'.	Harsh conditionality, coercion, and savage sanctions imposed. Increased risk of errors and fraud, and increased administration costs. No financial security for the poorest. Claimants at risk of deep indebtedness or destitution.	**UNCONDITIONAL** – no behavioural requirements are imposed. Obligation-free. Trusts people. Financial security.

systems

HELPS TO FULFIL OBJECTIVES	CHALLENGES AND FAQS	ADDITIONAL SUPPORTING ARGUMENTS
Liberates poorer partners from the financial dependence trap, and reduces inequality of power relationships in the home. More life choices – potential emancipation of *all* adults.	Can lead to substantial household economies of scale.	Removes disincentives that prevent people from sharing accommodation, including parents of dependent children who want to stay together. This could reduce the demand for single-adult housing.
Respects and values *all* individuals for their own sakes. Helps to reduce the *incidence* of income poverty, and to provide financial security. Protects the most vulnerable Helps to create a more just, united and inclusive society.	Why give it to rich people who don't need it? Would they benefit more from its introduction than the poorest?	It is more efficient (ie cheaper) to give BIs to all and to assess everyone once only pa for income tax. Claw back from the richest via a more progressive income tax system. Universal schemes are inclusive, popular and redistributive, and the rich tend to protect them for all.
Ends differentiation, stigma, division and low take-up. Less intrusive. Simpler, more efficient administration reduces costs and the risks of error and fraud. Not means-testing restores the incentives to work-for-pay. Absence of benefit tapers makes the new effective income tax rates less regressive. Complex work incentive effects. Wage rates will adjust.	Benefits should be differentiated because people's needs vary so much and are too complex for a single system. Surely means-testing is fairer? Will the BI act as a subsidy for employers?	Housing benefits and disability benefits would be granted *in addition to* BIs via separate systems, with new gateways where necessary. Other needs are better met via extended public services. A progressive income tax system would ensure a fairer distribution. Being undifferentiated, BIs would not compensate for lower wages – thus less incentive for employers to reduce wages.
Trusts adults with more control over the use of their own time. Income security – a right not to be destitute – reduces chronic stress, improving health and well-being. Quality of life. Reduces inequality of workplace power relationships – increases industrial democracy. Creative enterprise.	Why give 'something for nothing'? Reciprocity? Participation Income? What if some people give up working-for-pay? Free riders or minimal consumers?	Giving nothing shortens lives. A BI entitles people to necessities. Generosity to a recipient can induce reciprocity – and most people want to contribute to society. Also, most people want to work-for-pay for its health and other advantages. It could encourage redistribution between paid and unpaid work. Tolerate the few free riders.

Criticisms of the characteristics of the generic basic income

Some critics object to BIs being based on the individual, because cohabiting couples would receive double, despite the fact that they could survive on less. Yet, critics do not object to the fact that many non-cohabiting adults sharing accommodation are not penalised in this way. Household economies of scale would increase the incentives for people to share accommodation, including parents of dependent children who want to stay together. It could reduce the demand for single person housing. BIs based on the individual avoid the intrusive monitoring of people's relationships.

One can understand why critics ask, 'Why give BIs to rich people who don't need them?'. It seems to go against all sense of justice, and yet there are good reasons for doing so. To create a truly united and inclusive society, all must be part of it, including wealthier people. It has the added advantage that rich people tend to protect a system from which they benefit, thus also protecting it more effectively for the most vulnerable in society rather than by targeting them.

It is much more administratively efficient (cheaper) to give everyone a BI, and to assess individuals once only each year for income tax purposes, rather than for a second time with respect to benefits. Building progressivity into the income tax system could ensure that wealthy people do not profit unduly from the introduction of a BI system, while sharing in the feeling of financial security that a BI should provide. Many wealthier people must be concerned about the financial welfare of their offspring, now that fewer privileged jobs are guaranteed for them. Other universal systems, such as the NHS in the UK, are inclusive, popular and redistributive. Universality also helps to reduce the *incidence* of income poverty.

The criticism that too many people might give up working for pay altogether, without some form of means-testing and conditionality, is one that can be tested empirically. All the empirical evidence appears to confirm that most people want to work for pay, not just for the earnings, but for the health and social advantages that it confers – the opportunity to make friends, a structure to one's day or week, to learn new skills and many even enjoy job satisfaction. Few are likely to want to give up paid work altogether.

Unconditionality implies that people are trusted with more control over the use of their time. Some may choose less paid work in order to achieve a better work-life balance. Others may decrease their unpaid work and increase their contributions to the labour market. Thus, there could be a redistribution between paid and unpaid work.

'Unconditionality' seems to be the most problematic characteristic for some, asking 'Why give something for nothing?' and demanding reciprocity by participation in society as an authorised activity. There are several good reasons why people should receive an unconditional income:

- Everyone should be entitled to share in the natural resources and material heritage of their society, and to receive enough to cover their necessities as of right, otherwise their lives will be shortened for the 'crime' of being poor. There would still be incentives to earn and spend more;

- Inclusion and generosity together can induce a feeling of gratitude in recipients such that they feel moved to contribute to their society. Unconditionality means that they can choose their own method of doing so;

- Working for pay may not be an option for everyone.

Apart from the concern about work incentive effects, these criticisms are normative, based on values, which, for some, the countervailing arguments may not carry enough weight to change their opinions.

PART II

BI Schemes and Pilot Experiments from around the World

CHAPTER 4

BI pilot projects from North America

THE TERM 'BI PILOT projects' can include both experiments and other programs. The Mincome program was an experiment, but the Alaskan BI program is not. The Alaskan program fits the definition of an authentic BI, but the Mincome Program was technically a means-tested benefit experiment. Nevertheless, one can still learn from it. Its outcomes fall into the recognised patterns of emancipation, increased well-being and increased productivity. The degree of redistribution depends mainly on the generosity of the scheme and the method of financing it, which often tends to be the source of any difficulties – anticipated or real.

Mincome Program, Dauphin, Manitoba, Canada, 1974–79

The Mincome (Minimum Income) Program, in Dauphin, Manitoba, Canada, was an experiment that ran from 1974 to 1979. It ended abruptly when centre-right governments at both provincial (1977) and federal (1979) levels came into office. The problems of the 1970s – inflation, rising oil prices, higher interest rates and unemployment – became urgent and overtook the commitment to address poverty issues. No final report was made. The anonymised records of the five-year experiment were hastily packed away in 1,800 boxes, stored and lost for 30 years, until tracked down by

Professor Evelyn Forget (Forget, 2012) of Manitoba University. She was able to use a guest spot on a local radio station to invite participants to contact her, as a result of which several did so (Jourdan, 2013).

The objective of the experiment was to help households whose income dropped below the poverty line, and to ask whether people would stop working or work fewer hours if they were guaranteed an income? Would they be healthier, and would youngsters stay on at school for longer? The social assistance system in operation at that time was a Minimum Income Guarantee system which had very strong work disincentives, with a 100 per cent withdrawal rate of benefits, as earnings increased.

Dauphin was then a city of about 10,000 people serving a farming community. The whole population was in the experiment, in the sense that they were promised help if their income dropped below the poverty level. 1,000 families fell below the poverty line during the five-year experiment, comprising about one third of the population, and benefitted from a 'Mincome cheque'. This was not a true basic income in terms of the present-day concept, but rather a means-tested benefit program. It was targeted on low-income people (including seniors and disabled people), who received income support with a 50 per cent withdrawal rate. It was based on the family rather than the individual, and the amount varied according to family size. However, it was unconditional.

The cheques topped up household incomes to the poverty line:

> everyone was given the same base amount: 60 per cent of Statistics Canada's low-income cut-off. The cut-off varied depending on family size and where they lived. But in 1975, a single Canadian who was

considered low-income earned $3,386 on average (Lum, 2014).

For a family of two it was $4,907, and the corresponding figures in 2014 were $16,094 and $20,443.

The results had not been analysed by the original team, and are only now being analysed by Evelyn Forget, whose main interest is in the health benefits of the experiment. Nevertheless, it was established that few people had stopped working and hardly anyone with a full-time job reduced the hours that they worked. The design of the program with its 50 per cent withdrawal rate had created incentives for people to work, and provided a much more effective method of supplementing the incomes of the working poor. Married women took longer maternity leave. Adolescents, mainly boys, reduced the hours that they worked for pay. High school completion rates (grade 12) increased during the study. Many participants later expressed their gratitude for their educational opportunities in school or in job training.

Poverty had been reduced, aided by the financial predictability and stability of the Mincome support, keeping food on the table, bills paid, and the children in school. Researchers later said that they had not appreciated the depth of poverty experienced in Manitoba at that time. People were sick because they were poor. There were significant savings in health care costs. Forget found that

> hospitalisation rates fell by 8.5 per cent among subjects in the experiment relative to the controls. The reasons for that are reductions in 'accidents and injuries', less domestic abuse, and reductions in hospitalisation for mental health issues (Jourdan, 2013).

In other words, there was a measurable positive impact on the health care system.

Interest has risen in Canada again recently, and Ontario announced in its 2016 budget that it would design and implement a 'basic income' experiment. (It did not meet the requirements for an authentic BI experiment.) However, the newly elected provincial government announced in August 2018 that this experiment would be cancelled as from the end of March 2019, despite its assurances to the contrary during the election campaign.

Alaska, 1976–present

Alaska provides an example of a BI scheme that has survived for more than three decades. It is a genuine BI, being based on the individual, is universal for all who have resided in Alaska for at least a year, gives the same to everyone and is unconditional. It differs in two ways from proposals for the UK. First of all, the BIs are small in amount and are not intended as a social security system. Second, they are financed out of oil revenues accumulated and invested in the international stock market over the past 40 years.

In 1955, Alaska called a constitutional convention in advance of USA statehood in 1959, which led to the proclamation that all of the natural resources of Alaska belong to the state for the benefit of the people. Oil was then discovered in 1967 on its northern shore near Prudhoe Bay. The Alaska Permanent Fund (APF) was set up in 1976, due in large part to the single-minded determination of Jay Hammond, governor from 1974-82. At least 25 per cent of each year's oil *royalties* would be dedicated to the new APF. Hammond had hoped that at least 50 per cent of *the whole of the oil revenues*, and not just the royalties, would be dedicated, which would have been four times larger than was finally agreed. The APF was set up as a fund of income-producing investments, but there was no mention of how it would be used.

The Dividend Bill was passed in 1982, again due to Hammond's persistence. David Rose became the first executive director (1982–92) of the APF Corporation, the body created in 1980 to manage the fund and dividend. His goal was to follow the 'prudent investor rule', which set a precedent for it.

> These two books together lay out the long series of events between 1955 to 1992 that led to the APF being established in the Alaskan state constitution; the PFD [Permanent Fund Dividend] being established by law; the prudent investor rule being established by law and precedent; and all being protected by public opinion (Widerquist, 2011: 10).

Alaska has been able to distribute an annual dividend of between US$1,000 and US$2,000 each year since 1982 to everyone who had been resident in Alaska for the previous year, from the income from its sovereign wealth fund based on its oil revenues, the amount depending on the international financial markets.

Widerquist speculates on the outcome, had Governor Hammond had his way, and thus four times the amounts would have been dedicated to the APF. The best-case scenario could have led to a $400 billion fund in 2010:

> Suppose the state was able to withdraw 5 per cent each year, using half of it for dividends and half for the state's operating budget. That would produce a dividend of $15,000 per person a year and $10 billion for the state budget (Widerquist, 2011: 11).

The Alaska Dividend continues to be extremely popular. It

> distributes a yearly dividend to every man, woman and child in Alaska without any conditions whatsoever. It has helped Alaska maintain one of the lowest poverty

rates in the United States. It has helped Alaska become the most economically equal of all 50 states. And it has helped Alaska become the only US state in which equality has risen rather than fallen over the past 20 years. Certainly, Alaska is doing something right (Widerquist, 2010: 13).

Sadly, the happy situation of the APF Dividend is now under threat. In the past, Alaskans, in their wisdom, voted to use the rest of the income from the APF to finance public expenditure and to abolish all taxes, including sales and income tax. With the financial crisis in world markets, and the fall in the oil price, the return on the APF has dwindled, and Alaska is facing budget problems. Now there are proposals to divert the returns used to finance the APF Dividend in order to use it to fund public expenditure, rather than re-introduce taxes, such as income tax. This proposal would favour wealthier people at the expense of the poorest.

It will be noted that these two projects in North America occurred early in the chronology of late 20th century BI projects, and, indeed, the Alaskan one continues. Then not much happened for another two to three decades, when the action diverted to developing countries.

CHAPTER 5

Namibia and Iran

Namibia 2008–9

FROM 2004, THE NAMIBIAN BIG COALITION, comprising several organisations including the Council of Churches, the Namibian Union of Namibian workers, the Namibian NGO Forum and the Namibian Network of AIDS Service Organisations, campaigned to raise private donations from across Namibia and abroad, from both organisations and individuals, to finance an experiment.

The experiment took place in the two years from January 2008 to December 2009, in the small settlement of Otjivero-Omitara, a very low-income rural area in Namibia. Namibia is a low-to-middle income country, with average earnings per head of US$2,000 in 2009–10, but Namibia is one of the most unequal countries in the world, and about half of the population experiences severe poverty. Otjivero was at the lower income end, experiencing high levels of unemployment, poverty and frequent hunger.

Every individual man, woman and child who was resident in Otjivero on 31 July 2007, and who was under 60 years of age, was registered for the experiment. For children under the age of 21, a primary care-giver was provided, who by default was the mother. A sample of 50 out of some 200 households, comprising 930 residents, was selected, comprising individuals who would receive an unconditional income of N$100 (about US$12, or £7) per month for the two years (Haarman *et al*, 2008) (the cost for 930 residents at N$100 per month for 24 months will have been N$2,232,000 or £156,240, together with the costs of the researchers). A smart card was used to deliver the Basic Income Guarantee (BIG). This contained the name(s), ID number(s) and a picture, together with a microchip containing the date of birth, fingerprints, and information about the amount of the BIG and the history of their receipt of the grant.

A four-part method was used to collect data for the experiment:

- A baseline survey of the residents took place in November 2007.
- This was followed by a panel survey every six months thereafter until November 2009.
- Further information was provided by key informants, including the local nurse, police chief, shopkeepers and other local leaders.
- Detailed case studies of individuals were recorded.

The objective of the experiment was to achieve several goals, such as the eradication of poverty, universal primary education, and to promote gender equality and empower women (Haarman, 2008: 96). Even after as little as six months, significant changes were obvious. The percentage of malnourished children dropped from 42 to 17. More children attended school, and the drop-out rates reduced from 30–40 to 5 per cent. The schools were able to improve their teaching materials out of increased school revenues. Women's economic status improved and women were empowered through gaining more choices, enabling them to escape from abusive relationships and avoid having to earn money through sexual services. Health benefits were noted. More people were able to afford to visit the health clinic, leading to a reduction in cases of diarrhoea. Better nutrition for pregnant women improved maternal health. Improved nutrition and access to the clinic complemented the government's efforts to provide anti-retroviral therapy drugs to combat AIDS and HIV.

The majority of the participants increased their work, whether their hours of work were for pay, for profit or family gain, or from self-employment. The income in the community increased more than the total value of the grants, indicating that they had engaged in productive activities. BIG fostered local economic growth and development, including several small local enterprises. The number of crimes attributed to poverty declined. The experiment also had positive environmental effects, when access to electricity replaced cooking over firewood (Haarman, 2008).

The experiment demonstrated the undeniable beneficial effects of a BIG program. However, the government failed to extend the Otjivero program, let alone take steps to implement it elsewhere in Namibia.

Further information about the Namibian BIG Coalition and the BI pilot project can be found via www.bignam.org.

Iran 2010–6

In December 2010, Iran became the first country in the world to establish a nationwide basic income program. Interestingly, the scheme did not emerge by design, but by default: it was the by-product of an effort to reform an out-dated system of price subsidies that primarily concerned fuel products. A basic income proved to be the most practical way of compensating the population for the loss of subsidies that had been costing some US$100–120 billion a year (Tabatabai, 2012: 2).

Iran used to subsidise some food products, but mainly fuel, using its substantial oil revenues. Not only were these subsidies regarded as both inefficient and unfair, but it led to wasteful use of petrol that caused an increase in air pollution. It was decided to end these subsidies over a five-year period, gradually increasing fuel prices towards market rates, but to compensate the population by granting direct cash transfers instead, under their *Subsidy Reform Law* of January 2010. This became the main component of Iran's economic reform plan.

At first, the government tried to compensate the population via a needs-based system, but this caused a lot of friction and frustration as people complained that it, also, was unfair. In the end, the government decided to give the same amount to every Iranian. When the first phase of the reform process became operational on 19 December 2010, just over 80 per cent of the population of 75 million people started to receive 810,000 rials (about $80) every two months. However, the entitlements of all household members are payable to the head of the household alone, not to individual members, even if adult.

In the first year, about US$40 billion was paid out to households. Some 1–2 million households had decided not to claim the BI. 'The objective is twofold: improving economic efficiency through rationalisation of subsidised prices, and reducing income disparities through cash transfers' (Tabatabai, 2012: 2). Two effects have been noted. The prices of the previously subsidised commodities rose by one percentage point per month initially for the first year, but this was as anticipated. Secondly, there has been a decline in the consumption of fuel – again, to be expected.

The impact of the reform was expected to be egalitarian, because the subsidies withdrawn are in proportion to their consumption of the subsidised goods, and thus related to income size. However, the flat rate BI will have a greater impact on low-income people than on wealthier individuals. Iran has virtually established a regular *de facto* BI, not by design, but as a by-product of an attempt to transform an inefficient and unfair system of sharing the country's oil wealth by compensating its population for the loss of their subsidised fuel prices, which were contributing to pollution and increasing its carbon footprint.

Tabatabai draws some lessons from this experience. The source of funding for a BI scheme can be a major issue. In this case, the oil revenues provided the source, and the concern facing the population was that of making sure that they received their fair share. Tabatabai points out that this 'windfall' source of funding makes it easier to adopt a BI than if a rights or entitlement approach is made, with talk of reciprocity. He contrasts the Iranian BI scheme based on sharing the *current* oil revenues with Alaska's distributing part of the income from the *accumulated* sovereign wealth fund built up over the years, and which should last for longer.

A second lesson comes from the observation that the flow of funds in Iran is restricted in any given time period, and universality means that the share going to the poorer sections of the community is less than if eligibility had been targeted at them. A move has already started to urge higher income households to withdraw from the cash transfer scheme. He concludes that the

> success of the reform depends on the vast majority of the people feeling that they are not being cheated out of their fair share of the oil wealth.

Oil resources may be less controversial sources for funding a BI scheme initially, but they are not without their problems. Iran was hit by the fall in oil prices, and faced problems financing the cash transfer program, and so it proposed to withdraw this scheme from roughly one third of the wealthiest of the population. In fact, the program was ended in 2016, with cash subsidies being reserved for low-income citizens, despite evidence that the program had not undermined participation in work (BIEN, 2016; www.basicincome.org/Iran).

The BI programs in Iran and Alaska are similar in being financed from oil wealth, and being universal, uniform and unconditional. Despite being relatively small in amount, they were very popular with their residents.

CHAPTER 6

India's BI pilot experiments, 2011–13

THE OUTCOMES OF SOME BI pilot experiments in India in 2011–3 are particularly heart-warming, and illustrate the extra beneficial emancipatory effects of the scheme for women.

In spite of thousands of anti-poverty schemes having been launched across India over the years, poverty and deprivation are still visible everywhere. One of these schemes is the Public Distribution System that provides subsidised food (wheat, rice, sugar – and kerosene). The inefficiency of this system leads to immense material wastage and financial leakage, and prevents the intended beneficiaries from receiving their entitlements (Davala *et al*, 2015: 4).

Two BI pilot experiments were set up in Indore District in Madhya Pradesh (one of India's most under-developed regions), with financial help from the United Nations Children's Emergency Fund (UNICEF). The larger one started in June 2011 and ran until May 2012, and was then extended for a further six months. A sample was drawn up consisting of 50 villages, with about 100 households in each, from which eight villages were selected for receipt of the cash transfers, and a further 12 villages acted as controls.

The main activity was farm labouring. The Self-Employed Women's Association (SEWA) was already operative in half of the villages. All the men, women and children listed as usually resident in the household, that is, usually sleeping there for at least four nights a week, were eligible. Those who were already listed as resident at the beginning could form independent households within their village and remain in the sample. Newly married women and new babies could be added to the sample, but no others. This led to a total sample of 5,547 individuals who were eligible for the cash transfer in 938 households. There were another 1,096 households in the control villages, and altogether 11,231 individuals were involved in both experiment and control samples.

A basic income of 200 rupees per adult per month and 100 rupees per child was paid for the first 12 months, after which it was adjusted for inflation and increased by 50 per cent for the last six months. For the 30 per cent of the population whose income was below the poverty line, this represented about 30 per cent of their expenditure – on bare subsistence. For the 20 per cent of people whose income was above the poverty line, but who were still regarded as vulnerable, the BI represented less than 20 per cent of average income. The basic incomes replaced the food and fuel subsidies. Members of SEWA helped women to open bank accounts in the SEWA villages. A cash transfer team helped the other villagers to open their bank accounts.

A baseline survey or census was carried out in all 20 villages before the start of the pilot study, together with a Community Survey. An Interim Evaluation Survey was conducted half way through the pilot, and a Final Evaluation Survey and another Community Survey carried out at the end. A Post-Final Evaluation was made some months after the end of the pilot. The survey data was supported by 100 case studies of families, and specialist information was collected from designated key informants (Davala *et al*, 2015: 40).

The smaller of the two pilot experiments in Madhya Pradesh involved one tribal village of 127 households with 756 residents, and one similar control village of 97 households with 817 inhabitants. This experiment lasted from February 2012 to January 2013. Adults received Rs 300 per month each, and children Rs 150 each, paid to the mother. The average amount received per household was Rs 1,276 per month. A similar set of surveys was carried out as for the larger project.

The results were very positive. The outcomes fell into three areas – an emancipatory effect, improvement in well-being, and an increase in productivity. The cash transfer payments had an emancipatory effect on many who had a low status in their communities, even apart from the caste system. Women were the immediately obvious examples in a society where the women were second-class citizens with no citizenship rights (even in high caste households), with no identity, and no empowerment. Their first problem was to establish that they existed, in order to open a bank account. This could take several weeks, but SEWA helped in the SEWA villages.

The individualisation of the BI meant that, for the first time, women had some control over their lives and influence in the household. Both men and women agreed that women had been major beneficiaries of the advantages offered by the cash transfers. BI was emancipatory for two other groups – disabled people and the elderly, who tended to be marginalised within their households when food and money were tight. Both groups benefitted from better nutrition and easier access to healthcare services. Another example of the emancipatory nature of BIs occurred when it helped some families, who, by pooling their BIs, were able to buy a family member out of bonded labour.

Well-being covers such matters as living conditions, nutrition, health and education. It was found that some of the cash transfers were used by the villagers to improve their living standards by pooling them to install latrines in their dwellings, which had a knock-on effect on the health of its members. A second improvement was that of many households installing a tube well for irrigation, or having a private tap or pump in the house for drinking water, the effects of which would continue after the end of the project. Another improvement came from the increased use of electricity for cooking and lighting, and others were able to make repairs to their dwellings, while a few built new ones. Some households bought useful assets such as furniture, or items of transport such as bicycles, scooters or motorbikes, or mobile phones, an electric fan, a TV, or changed to using modern methods of protection against mosquitoes.

Improvements in nutrition came about by people being able to widen their diets to include fresh vegetables and fruit, milk, eggs and fish: 'the establishment of a fishing cooperative in the tribal village led to a transformation of the diet of the villagers' (Davala, 2015: 96). Some of the improved nutrition was directly due to their being able to buy food with cash rather than credit and thus avoid the high interest rates. Others were able to buy in bulk and avoid the time and transport costs of frequent trips to the market. It had a substantial effect on children, in that height-for-age and weight-for-age distributions increased towards the standards recommended by the World Health Organisation, and this improvement was even more marked for girls than for boys.

The health effects that were observed

> may be four-fold. First, basic income may improve resilience to sickness... Second, it may improve preparedness, the ability to respond in a timely

> manner to an illness or accident... Third, there may be a reduction of debt incurred to fund medical expenses... Fourth... is that besides the effect of cash or income in itself there is a powerful positive effect of income security (Davala *et al*, 2015: 99-100).

The villagers preferred to use private healthcare services rather than public health facilities, but this was mainly on account of the poor quality of the services provided by the latter.

Basic incomes also had a significant effect on education:

> it may enable some families to spend on essential or useful items that enable their children to go to school more easily or cheaply. It may facilitate better eating habits... giving children more energy and health, and thus making it more likely they will go to school and be able to learn properly while there (Davala *et al*, 2015: 115).

It might also enable families to send their children to a better school, or to pay for private tuition outside school. It could also release the children from working on their family farm or from other paid labour. Basic incomes were associated with increased enrolment, attendance and performance at school, and more school-related spending, on uniforms, shoes, tuition fees, books and transport to school:

> a particularly encouraging sign was that expenditure on schooling for girls was decidedly higher among households receiving the basic income. This effect was even greater among those in SEWA villages, where spending on girls' schooling increased by over 100 per cent...' (Davala *et al*, 2015: 119).

Basic incomes were also found to have a positive effect on work, productivity and growth 'in and around agriculture and small-scale production of basic goods and services' (Davala *et al*, 2015: 137). It reduced child labour both in waged work and on the farm, in favour of education.

Time spent on labour can be divided into its components: caring for children and others, 'housework', own-account work for oneself or for family, non-farming income-earning activity, and labour for wages or some non-monetary payment. Participants in the pilot studies often had a main and a second labour activity, the two sources of income together giving greater protection. The BI often enabled that dual activity to occur, especially for women. There was also a shift to own-account work from the casual wage labour that had involved competing for limited opportunities. This enabled them to strengthen their bargaining power in the market for wage labour. Women were the primary beneficiaries of growth in secondary economic activities. The individualised cash transfer led to independent work opportunities. Several groups of women pooled their BIs to buy sewing machines to make clothes for their families and for others.

The cash transfer enabled the villagers to farm their land more intensively. They bought assets: small or large livestock, seeds, fertiliser, pesticides, tools and equipment, tube wells and electric pumps for irrigation, the effect of which would continue after the end of the experiment. In the tribal village, a cooperative fish farm was set up, which helped to improve their own and others' diets. Together with their improved nutrition and health, the BI provided a safety valve. The steady predictable income reduced the adverse shock of temporary unemployment, and people were less likely to default on debt payments. This also had an emancipatory effect, as the villagers had greater control over their lives. The economic value of the positive effects exceeded the value of the transfer.

The pilot experiment was such a success that several political parties wanted to get in on the act before the election in 2014. In their haste, they were intending to reduce the subsidies before the infrastructure of individualised bank accounts had been set up, and the people were able to receive their transfers, which would have been an absolute disaster (Standing, 2013).

> In 2014, the Indian population elected a new government, the first with an absolute majority of seats for 30 years... Reforms should start soon and be what is called 'evidence-based'. All the old policies seem set for review' (Davala et al, 2015:196).

The three areas into which the outcomes fell – an emancipatory effect, improvement in well-being, and an increase in productivity – are precisely three of the objectives identified in chapter 3 to which an income maintenance system, such as a BI scheme, can contribute. The same broad outcomes could be expected from BI pilot experiments in Scotland or the UK. However, now attention switches to Europe.

CHAPTER 7
Some recent BI experiments and proposals

Finland, 2017-8

THE ANNOUNCEMENT IN November 2015, that Finland would dedicate 20m euros towards a BI experiment over two years, starting in 2017 (the first large-scale trial in Europe), was greeted with a flurry of excitement. Although the previous BI experiments have provided useful results, it is important to be able to assess the effects of BI on a society which already has a well-developed social security system.

The four objectives behind the trial were:

- To overhaul Finland's Social Security system taking account of changes in the labour market;
- To make it more effective in terms of providing incentives to work for pay and avoiding the poverty trap;
- To simplify the administration system, reducing bureaucracy and administration costs; and
- To evaluate the effects on members of different population groups.

It was anticipated that the experiment would involve four different schemes – (i) a full BI, (ii) a partial BI, (iii) a BI delivered in the form of NIT and TCs, where the delivery is through the income tax system, and (iv) a participation income given to unemployed people.

However, a preliminary report published in March 2016 concluded that there were good reasons why only the 'partial BI' scheme could go ahead. In fact, the Finnish experiment is a *targeted* partial BI scheme. A random sample was selected, comprising 2,000 people, between the ages of 25 and 58, who were unemployed in November 2016, from a population of 175,000 unemployed people, who would act as a control group. From January 2017, the sample subjects were sent 560 euros per month out of the blue, continuing for two years until the end of December 2018. It replaced their unemployment benefit. They will keep the BI, even if they find work. The government hoped that it would encourage the unemployed to take on part-time work and reduce the anxiety of losing their benefits.

The names of the recipients had not been released but the media had been able to identify a few of them, and, after an interview, had issued an unofficial report that the experiment was going well – based on a sample of one.

This experiment illustrates two aspects of many proposed BI experiments – that, often, they are not able to be as ambitious as initially intended, because of financial constraints, and secondly, that they do not end up as authentic BI schemes, where the sample would have covered all income levels. Nevertheless, these situations have provided unconditional cash payments to their participants and much useful information can be gained from studying their effects on health, work incentives and the status of women, among other things.

One of the unusual aspects of this project is that the subjects are not being asked to complete questionnaires, since the government does not wish to influence the outcome of the experiment. The analysis will be carried out using data from administrative registers.

The results of a preliminary analysis of the data from the first year of the experiment, published in early 2019, found two outcomes: the BI did not make much difference to the recipients' labour force participation, but they were very much happier than before.

Scotland, 2017–present

In November 2015, in its report, *Fairness Matters*, the Fairer Fife Commission expressed its hope that Fife Council would select a town to test and evaluate a basic income pilot experiment. A year later, on 26 November 2016 in Govan, Glasgow, at the launch of the newly-formed charity, Citizen's Basic Income Network Scotland (CBINS), local councillor, Matt Kerr, announced the intention of Glasgow City Council to host a BI experiment also. North Ayrshire was quick to follow. Meetings were held in these three local authority areas, supported by the Royal Society for Arts (RSA) in Scotland, to discuss the possibilities and to inform both councillors and the public as to what might be involved, with very positive reactions. In August 2017, the City of Edinburgh Council announced its wish to be involved.

In its *Program for Government* in early September 2017, the Scottish Government earmarked £250,000 as seed corn finance to support the planning phase during the period from April 2018 to April 2020. The Citizen's Basic Income Feasibility Study Steering Group comprises officers from each of the four Councils, supported by NHS Health Scotland and the Improvement Service (www.basicincome.scot). On 29 March 2018, the Steering Group submitted an *Application for Funding* to the Scottish Government for the planning phase. The application was approved in May. A Cross Party Group on Basic Income was formally registered at Holyrood in June 2018. The Steering Group published its thoroughly researched interim report in October 2019.

CBINS can make an important contribution to educating opinion-formers and the public about the desirability and feasibility of BI schemes, and encouraging them to engage with their elected representatives, who will have a role to play to progress the Feasibility Study to its implementation stage.

Even if the proposal is approved in 2020 for a BI pilot experiment with a minimum of three-years duration, together with a preparation year, the results would only become available in 2025 at the earliest, and it could all take much longer. Even if the UK government agreed to devolve the necessary fiscal powers to Holyrood immediately, the earliest that a BI scheme could be implemented nationwide in Scotland would be the following year, and it could take between five and ten years before the aspired-to model was finally achieved.

Kenya, 2017–30

Several other BI pilots are being planned or started across Europe and North America. However, one of the most interesting is taking place in Kenya, privately financed by GiveDirectly (www.givedirectly.org/basic-income), a UK charity.

Three hundred villages have been randomly assigned to one of four groups. Two hundred villages (about 26,000 people) have been allocated to three treatment groups, with 100 villages acting as the control group. These are saturation samples with the recipients receiving an authentic universal, unconditional BI based on the individual, to the value of US$22 (20 euros) per month. Forty villages comprise one treatment group, receiving the BI for 12 years, another 80 villages receive it for two years and the final 80 villages receive a lump sum equivalent to 24 months of regular BI.

The objectives of the project are to investigate:

- How important is the guarantee of future transfers for risk-taking, such as starting a business?
- What difference does it make to have the BI as a lump sum, rather than as a regular payment?
- Other matters, such as 'economic status', time-use, risk-taking and gender relations.

The first village received its BIs in October 2016, and the rest were started in September 2017. This is a long-term project exploring some interesting aspects of BI.

Republic of Korea, 2019-present

Since the tragic war that divided the East Asian peninsula of Korea in the 1950s, South Korea has enjoyed an enviable rate of economic growth, but also experienced massive poverty. However, Governor Lee of Gyeonggi Province (the largest in the country comprising a quarter of its population) has asked the question 'For whom are the benefits of economic growth? In April 2019, he inaugurated a BI project for all 175,000 24-year olds in the province, who will each receive one million Korean Won (about £750) in quarterly instalments for one year. The project was launched with a celebratory fair and a conference attended by international speakers.

PART III

Practical Issues: Designing and Costing a Basic Income Model

A basic income is a periodic cash payment unconditionally delivered to all on an individual basis, without means test or work requirement.

BASIC INCOME EARTH NETWORK (BIEN)

CHAPTER 8

Designing a BI model

THERE IS BROAD CONSENSUS about BIEN's set of six revised characteristics. These merely define a particular *class* of income maintenance systems. Many different BI schemes, or *models*, are possible within the class, each being the product of a set of the prioritised secondary objectives, assumptions and constraints of its devisor. These should be made explicit at the start of the design process. There is no consensus about the design of particular BI models. Several have already been put forward by different researchers, but their intentions have not always been clear. All authentic BI models can be expected to contribute to the broad objectives laid out in chapter 3 above; the extent to which they achieve this depends on their level of generosity.

Part III presents some of the matters that should be considered when designing a BI model for the UK, but it could also be useful for other countries with well-developed Social Security systems. It provides the opportunity to think about the issues. There is no consensus on what the answers should be. Where an answer is provided here, it is merely to indicate that at least one answer is possible, but other viable solutions could also emerge.

A *full BI* would be high enough and stable enough to enable a single person to enjoy a dignified, if modest, standard of living, and to participate in social, cultural and public life. A *partial BI* would need to be topped up by other income, usually earnings. Even a partial BI could contribute to the broad objectives to some extent, but the effects increase with the generosity of the scheme. A *child BI* would be granted to a dependent child to be administered on her/his behalf by the primary care-giving parent (as now in the UK).

When designing a BI model, the main tasks are to decide on criteria for eligibility, at what level to pitch the BIs, whether there should be differences between various age groups, and, if so, how much to allocate to each group, and how to treat current NI and SA benefits. It should also consider some administrative matters, such as setting up a database, implementation, delivery, monitoring and compliance, and identify potential sources of finance for the BIs. These are considered in chapters 9–11.

How much of the UK Social Security system could a BI eventually replace?

It must be emphasised that the BI could replace much of the current Social Security system, but not the rest of the welfare state – that is, it would not replace public welfare services, such as health, social care or education.

It has been claimed that the needs and lives of people are far too complex to be served by a single, or over-simplified, income maintenance system, and this is true.

People with disabilities would receive (preferably enhanced) needs-based disability benefits via a parallel but separate system, as now. It is essential that people with disabilities define and propose this system for themselves, rather than able-bodied people prescribing what they think is right for them. Elder-Woodward and Duffy (2018) express concerns that the needs of disabled people could be over-looked within a BI system and that they could end up worse off than now. Not only should people with disabilities receive, *in addition to* their BIs, tax-exempt payments to cover the extra costs that many of them incur, such as those for mobility, care, special equipment, special diets, extra fuel and laundry. But they should also receive sufficient benefits, including a personal budget, to enable them to achieve independent living and the ability to participate in society wherever possible, based on self-directed support. Emancipation for all, including disabled people, should be one of the aims of the BI and related cash transfer payment systems.

Where there is a wide variety of house prices and rents across a country, such as in the UK, it is impossible to include a uniform element in the BI to cover housing costs, without leaving poorer people in the more expensive areas with too little to cover their housing needs. This is a housing policy problem, not one caused by Social Security, and so the solution lies in changing the UK housing policy. In the meantime, a parallel, but separate, individualised, means-tested Housing Benefit (HB) and Council Tax Support system will have to be retained (but preferably with a less steep withdrawal taper than the current 65 per cent for HB). This implies that means-testing certainly could not be completely ended before a new housing policy has been implemented, even if a full BI system is in place. Thus, 'After Housing Costs have been deducted' (AHC) versions of poverty benchmarks should be selected for all BI systems which do not include a housing cost element.

The UK system of childcare benefits is very complex and one of the most expensive in Europe. Childcare provision would also have to be separate from the BI scheme. It would be more efficient if childcare services were adequately state-funded, and if nurseries for all 2–4-year-olds could be provided in primary schools eventually.

Eligibility and migration

A BI is universal, not targeted on a specific section of the population, such as a particular income group. However, a BI cannot be literally universal, nor is it even likely to be world-wide in the near future. The population must be defined and eligibility criteria are required, based on geographical area and legal rights. So, who would be eligible, and who would be excluded?

'Citizenship' is a multi-faceted concept, involving civil, political, social and economic rights and responsibilities, which could be difficult to apply. Many BI advocates recommend that eligibility should be based on a residency qualification, such as having the legal right to permanent residence, including being subject to its taxation laws.

A further criterion would have to be fulfilled, such as a minimum period of continuous legal and physical residence in the country prior to receipt of its BI. It is also reasonable to require all those in receipt of a BI to maintain a continuing physical presence in the BI-awarding country for the majority of each subsequent year, in order to contribute to the society and economy that is supporting them.

Although much of the Social Security system would be decriminalised, some monitoring of the residency conditions would be required, in addition to checking whether an individual was claiming to be more than one person, or a parent-with-care was claiming for more children than live with her.

The problem of a residency condition for homeless people and travellers would still need to be addressed. In France, they have access to a Poste Restante address, and the banks are required to provide a basic bank account for everyone, including homeless people. All state benefits are paid on the same day of the month in France, which can aid budgeting.

Some people suggest that prisoners should forfeit their BIs. However, this would be the thin end of the wedge of finding reasons for withdrawing a person's right to BI. Some of a prisoner's BI could contribute to their 'board and lodge', but maybe part of their BIs should be accumulated for when they leave prison to help them to avoid recidivism.

The country of origin would have to make arrangements for their residents who work abroad on short-term contracts, and for their students taking a gap year or studying abroad.

Criteria would also be needed to address specific residence situations including the following four groups of people:

- Millions of citizens do not exercise their legal right to permanent residence in their country of origin, but have relocated abroad, and to whom their country of origin would not expect to grant a BI. However, if, or when, they wished to return home, they too would have to fulfil the further eligibility criteria.

- Migrants to the UK from parts of the EU, depending on the UK's relationship with the EU.

- Asylum seekers, who seek refugee status on account of persecution, war or natural disasters in their own countries. Compassion requires that they are treated more humanely in the UK than currently, and that the process of assessing their claims for refugee status is speeded up. A BI during this process could avoid the risk of destitution.

- Other migrants who do not fall within any of the above categories.

The main factor influencing the rate of economic migration is the difference between the wage-rates in the destination and source countries. However, migration has both positive and negative consequences for both host and origin countries. Reluctant migrants would prefer to stay in their own countries and cultures to build up their home economies, if opportunities allowed. This might help to stem the brain drains from the source countries.

A well-administered international BI system, that delivered a BI to each individual, with no opportunity for corruption, might help to redistribute incomes from developed to developing countries more effectively than the current systems of foreign aid, and create a more optimistic environment in the latter countries.

If an individual who wished to move from his own BI-issuing jurisdiction to another BI-issuing domain were to be eligible for only the lesser BI of the two domains, might this discourage mass migration in the future?

Poverty-prevention benchmarks

If preventing poverty eventually is one of the objectives of the BI system (even if the system is to be implemented gradually), then reference should be made to the following poverty benchmarks.

The EU's official poverty benchmark was adopted briefly into UK law in the Child Poverty Act, 2010–16. The couple household is treated as standard and given a weight of 1.00. The benchmark used to be based on 0.5 of the mean, but currently it is defined as '0.6 of median equivalised net household income' for a nation's population. The DWP's annual *Households Below Average Income* (HBAI) publishes four potential poverty benchmarks for the previous fiscal year. Unfortunately, the latest information published in 2019 relating to the fiscal year 2017–8, is already too out-of-date to be really useful for determining BIs for the fiscal year two years later in 2020–21. HBAI gives figures for both Before Housing Costs (BHC) are deducted and After Housing Costs

(AHC) are deducted. The AHC version must be used for BIs when Housing Benefit is administered as a separate system.

Table 8.1 EU official poverty benchmarks for the UK, based on the couple

Based on 2017–18 data £ pw	MEAN	MEDIAN
Proportion for a couple	0.5	0.6
BHC	**613.00**	**507.00**
Poverty benchmark for a couple	306.50	304.20
0.67 for 1st adult	205.35	203.81
0.33 for other adults aged 14 or over	101.15	100.39
0.20 for child aged 0–13	61.30	60.84
AHC	**536.00**	**437.00**
Poverty benchmark for a couple	268.00	262.20
0.58 for 1st adult	155.44	152.08
0.42 for other adults aged 14 or over	112.56	110.12
0.20 for child aged 0–13	53.60	52.44

None of the poverty benchmarks is perfect, and the official one has four obvious drawbacks:

- It is based on the median, which is not as good a measure of prosperity in society as the *mean*. The median of the skewed income distribution is always less than the mean, but, according to Table 8.1, 0.6 of the median has been roughly equal to 0.5 of the mean.

- It uses *net disposable weekly income* from all sources *after* income tax, National Insurance contributions and other deductions have been made, and benefits have been received. This implies that some redistributive measures have already taken place, which could influence the poverty benchmark. Certainly, the mean of net incomes will be less than the mean of gross incomes. It is more important to know the distribution of *gross* (pre-tax-and-benefits) incomes, to be able to identify those who are most at risk of poverty, and to address that problem directly rather than make piecemeal changes to measures that are already in place.

- The EU poverty threshold is based on equivalised *household* income, on the assumption that all individuals in the household benefit equally from the combined income of the household. This is a heroic assumption that is clearly unsafe. Household measures of income mask and ignore intra-household inequality. The distribution of gross income of *individuals*, including those who have no source of gross income, is needed to give a more accurate picture of those at risk of poverty.

- In the UK, the information relating to a previous fiscal year is already more than *a year out-of-date* when published in June, for decision-making for the following fiscal year. This is particularly misleading when the economy is suffering from inflation. A figure for the mean gross income of individuals for the previous *calendar year* is available by late summer, on which to base the levels of the BIs in the following fiscal year.

An alternative poverty benchmark is proposed here, based on:

- the *mean* of the distribution of
- *gross* incomes (*prior to* the deduction of taxes, NICs or benefit withdrawals, and the addition of benefits, including state pensions), of
- *individuals*, for

- a *calendar year*, with the information being published within nine months of the previous year end, as now.

I refer to this measure as **Y-BAR** (pronounced 'why-bar').

The proposed poverty benchmark for an adult would be 0.5 of Y-BAR for BHC estimates and 0.4 for AHC ones, with Y-BAR rounded up to the nearest multiple of £1.25. The child benchmark would be 0.25 and 0.20 for BHC and AHC respectively.

Table 8.2 A new poverty benchmark, based on the individual

	£ pw	UK	SCOT
Y-BAR*	2018	**472.50**	**405.00**
BIs for 2020–21			
BHC 0.50 for all adults 0.25 for a child		236.25 118.13	202.50 101.25
AHC 0.40 for all adults 0.20 for a child		189.00 94.50	162.00 81.00

* Rounded up to the nearest multiple of £1.25.

The **Minimum Income Standards** (MIS) comprises another set of poverty benchmarks for the UK, which is calculated by focus groups, and provides detailed estimates for 11 different household configurations (see column 5 in Table 8.6). Both BHC and AHC versions are available. It provides more generous poverty-prevention levels than the EU benchmark.

Van Parijs *et al* (2017: 11) 'suggest picking an amount of the order of one fourth of its current GDP per capita', which allowing for age-related differences 'would be an average rather than a uniform amount'. Based on the 2018 figure for GDP in the UK, this would yield an average BI of £154.46 pw for 2020–21.

A full BI for the UK could then be defined in terms of the AHC version of the poverty benchmark chosen. All of these poverty benchmarks are measures based on incomes. Gross income sources include:

- earnings, wages, salaries and bonuses;
- earnings from self-employment;
- share schemes and options from one's employer;
- company perquisites (perks);
- pensions, occupational and personal;
- royalties;
- interest from banks, building societies and other financial institutions;
- dividends;
- capital gains on the sale of shares and other assets;
- rental income from properties;
- gifts and legacies.

At what levels should the BIs be set?

BIEN does not define the level of a full BI, but, on the whole, it is expected to cover only basic needs, such as: food; alcohol and tobacco; clothing; household goods, insurance and other services; fuel and other housing costs; personal goods and services; travel costs; and social and cultural participation (*Minimum Income Standards*).

Some people query why an element for 'alcohol and tobacco' is included in this list, when they can be detrimental to health, and many wealthier people have been able to overthrow these habits. However, it is not for the privileged to dictate to people suffering from multiple deprivations that they should forego these comforts before they have been able to sort out other more pressing worries, such as coping with the chronic stress and anxiety of living with the never-ending threat of impending destitution hanging over them.

BI levels are uniform, except that differences based on age are acceptable, with a child usually receiving less than an adult.

Readers are invited to consider the questions below, using them to design their own BI models and complete the tables in the Work Book presented in Appendix B.

Full BIs

- Would pensioners and working age adults receive the same level of full BI, or who would have more?

- Should young adults (aged 16–18, 19–24) receive less than other working age adults (following current UK Social Security practice), or the same as, or more than, other working age adults?

- The EU official poverty benchmark treats 14–15-year-olds the same as second adults in a household. What level of BI should be given to 14–15-year-olds?

- Define a full Child BI such that the sum of BIs for all within the household meets the chosen poverty benchmark for the relevant household configuration (see Table 8.6), given that the adult BI levels have been set already.

- Will two or more adults sharing accommodation (including cohabiting couples), receive more than they 'need'? Yes, certainly with a full BI (and also with relatively generous partial BIs). This is called Household Economies of Scale (HES). But HES can provide an incentive for adults to share accommodation and thus reduce demand for single-person housing. Accepting HES as a possible consequence of BI schemes also acknowledges that sharing accommodation is not always easy – it can be stressful and compromises often have to be made.

While full BIs may be the goal, gradual implementation is likely to involve partial BIs for working age adults.

- Where partial BIs are involved, *is there a case for differentiation in order to protect families with children and financially-vulnerable adults* (who are discriminated against in the labour market, and whom a compassionate society would not compel to top up their BIs from earnings) – Lone Parents (LPs) and other primary care-giving parents (Parents with Care [PwC]), and disabled people?

- Should all PwCs including LPs be granted a premium to top up their partial BIs to full BIs? Note that all PwCs would have to receive the same level of BIs in order to avoid the intrusive monitoring that would accompany differentiating between their statuses. Granting a premium to all PwCs to top up a partial BI to a full one, would be straightforward administratively, because these would be the people to whom Child BIs would be paid, to administer on behalf of the child, as now with Child Benefit. This would also reduce the effect of HES on couples.

- Is there a minimum acceptable level of partial BI that would, for instance, enable an adult to volunteer as an *unpaid* carer for a family member or friend without the risk of destitution?

Carer's Allowance, paid in addition to the BI, would recognise the special value of caring. The caregiver for a disabled person would have to be registered and their emoluments could be organised via the separate Disability Benefits system. Other paid carers would receive their remuneration from the agencies that would provide care packages for those who need them

It soon becomes obvious that a full BI resolves the problems of financially-vulnerable adults, not just lone parents and unpaid volunteer carers, but also of other single adults who are unable to work to top up a partial BI for a variety of reasons. Ultimately, the most compassionate approach would be to grant full BIs to all adults.

Treatment of NI benefits

The basic state pensions (BSPs) – the State Retirement Pension (SRP), and the more recent Single Tier Pension (STP) introduced in 2016 for those who have just reached pension-retirement age – are NI benefits, and their levels depend on the individual's contribution record. Pensioners are entitled to apply to top up their BSPs with means-tested Pension Credit, although many eschew this course of action to avoid the humiliation involved. These BSPs would be replaced by full BIs.

Under the EU/UK poverty benchmark, based on 2017–18 figures, UK pensioners would have been entitled to a maximum of £152.08 pw in 2020–21. The UK already pays out more than this, as indicated in Table 8.3. In order to fulfil the promise that no poor person would be worse off financially as a result of the introduction of the BI system, every pensioner would receive a BI equal to the Pension Credit for a single pensioner or the STP level. This should prevail for a fully fiscally-devolved Scotland. However, if the proposed new benchmark were to be adopted for the UK, all pensioners would receive 0.4 of Y-BAR, ie £189 pw.

Table 8.3 Single pensioner benefit levels

For 2020–21	£ pw	UK	SCOT BI	UK BI
Y-BAR*	2018		405.00	472.50
0.4 Y-BAR			162.00	189.00
EU poverty benchmark		152.08		
SRP		134.25		
Pension Credit level		173.75	173.75	
STP		175.20	175.20	

* Rounded up to the nearest multiple of £1.25.

Some pensioners might prefer to keep their STPs or their SRPs (while receiving the tax-free top-up), because NI pensions are portable if pensioners wish to retire to other parts of the world, but they are not necessarily inflation-proofed. The BIs would normally be more restrictive.

All extra contributory state pensions should be honoured, such as the State Earnings Related Pension Scheme (SERPS), and State Second Pension (S2P), for which contributions to the state scheme have been opted when faced with a choice of contributions to a state or a private scheme.

Maternity benefits could be replaced by initiating the child BIs and the PwC premium for new mothers at, or backdated to, the 13th week of pregnancy. Similarly, the BIs of deceased persons could be extended for six months after death and paid into their estates to help with funeral expenses.

No other NI benefits should be withdrawn unless a BI serving the same function and of an equivalent amount has been implemented (such as for contributory Jobseeker's Allowance and contributory Employment and Support Allowance).

Treatment of Social Assistance benefits

Some BI proposals state that SA benefits will be reduced, cut, abolished, removed or replaced by the BIs, but do not describe the intended method. The UK's SA system is so complex, that it would be impossible to ensure that every situation for which a benefit was granted was also covered by a BI. It is essential to retain the SA benefit system in place to ensure that claimants do not receive less as a result of the implementation of the BI scheme. It also gives administrators the opportunity to ensure that all is working as planned and to identify any unintended consequences.

If the BI is taken into account, it will reduce claimants' entitlement to MTBs. If the BI is less than the amount of the MTB, a claimant would be no better off financially than under the existing SA system. No poor person should be made worse off as the result of the introduction of a BI system, but equally it would be preferable if those who rely completely on benefits could be made better off. There are two ways in which a claimant could be better off financially. One is to increase the BIs. The other is to grant the BIs wholly and completely in addition to existing benefits, and thus they would not be taken into account for MTBs. Spicker puts forward the suggestion of giving every man, woman and child a BI of £100 per month in this way, which could make a real difference to poor people (Spicker, 2019). In all of these cases, people on higher incomes are also receiving the BIs, but a progressive income tax system could ensure that wealthier recipients do not profit overall from the introduction of the BI scheme. That is explored in chapters 10 and 11.

It is possible that a main earner, who formerly received benefits on behalf of his/her 'dependents', could find him/herself with less income, and yet the total income of the household could have increased, with the 'dependents' now receiving their own BIs directly.

As the level of the BIs is increased, the claimants will be floated off means-testing, and the MTB system should eventually wither away, leaving just a residual scheme comprising some **retained benefits**, for which a BI is not a good substitute. These could be identified at this later stage, and, if necessary, appropriate substitutes could be devised for them. They would include the Social Fund and the Scottish Welfare Fund (including Cold Weather Payments), which provide for emergencies such as fire or flood; Winter Fuel Payments; a residual NI scheme for those who are eligible for the UK State Retirement Pension, but who live abroad; SERPS and S2P; and Guardian's Allowance. Other retained benefits include the separate but parallel (enhanced) Care and Disability Benefit system, and the Housing Benefit system.

The costs of these retained benefits, together with the costs of administering the BIs, comprise a margin which must be added to the cost of the BIs (the sum of gross transfers), to calculate the grand total cost of the reformed Social Security system. These are calculated in Table 8.4.

Some of the current MTBs carry extra components representing the needs of adult dependents and children, housing and disability benefits, and childcare costs. Obviously, the BIs will take care of the adults and dependent children. There will be parallel but separate systems of Housing Benefit and Disability Benefits. State-funded nurseries could be a much more effective way of contributing to parents' childcare needs, than by individual cash grants, which has tended to be associated with increased childcare prices.

Table 8.4 Costs of the components of the margin for 2020–21, based on data available in 2019

REF	Components of MARGIN	UK £m	Scot £m
	Administration costs	7,673	554
GTLQ	Social Fund, Scottish Welfare Fund, including Cold Weather Payments	2,115	176
	Winter Fuel Payments	1,986	166
	NI Retirement abroad	4,115	343
	SERPS and S2P	18,210	1,518
CSDH	Guardians' Allowances	450	38
EKY5	Care Allowances, Enhanced by 50%	8,600 / 4,300	717 / 358
EKY6	Disability benefits Enhanced by 50%	9,229 / 4,615	769 / 385
CTML	Rent Rebates (Local Auths)	5,144	429
GCSR	Rent Allowances (Private)	15,566	1,297
	TOTAL for MARGIN, £m	**82,003**	**6,750**
QWMF	Total Income £bn	1,634	115
	Margin divided by Income	**0.0502**	**0.0587**

The reference codes (REF) are those from *The Blue Book*, 2019. For Scotland, all but the administration costs and Total Income are estimated as one twelfth of that for the UK. The sources are given in the 'Main sources of data for the UK' section at the end of the book.

There is also a further system of passported benefits to which claimants are entitled on account of their receipt of one of the main MTBs (Income Support [IS], Jobseeker's Allowance [JSA], Employment and Support Allowance [ESA], Universal Credit [UC], or Pension Credit [PC]). These include items such as free school lunches, discretionary payments for school uniforms, discretionary fuel payments, legal aid, or free transport to visit close family members in prison, which would be lost under a BI system. One way of making some of these available could be through extended welfare services. Pensioners in the UK currently hold free bus passes, which reduces the isolation of many elderly poor people, takes the cars of others off the roads, and provides a ready market for local bus services, which keeps them economically viable. Extending these free services to all sections of the public could solve some of the problems. Similarly, free school lunches for all pupils could avoid the stigmatising of children from poor families. Other methods of providing access to the other services would have to be devised.

It soon becomes clear that even a generous BI scheme could not replace the whole of the SA system. There could be a hierarchical system of benefits in which BIs would provide a foundational income. There could be some state-funded second pensions, some retained MTBs and other SA benefits, together with parallel but separate systems of means-tested housing benefits and needs-based Disability Benefits.

Examples of a BI scheme for a fully fiscally-devolved Scotland and for the UK

The tables below are based on the same partial BI example for both Scotland and the UK. Table 8.5 calculates the cost in terms of £m. Table 8.6 shows how much each household type could receive from a fully fiscally-devolved Scotland. The Workbook in Appendix B provides the opportunity for readers to devise and cost their own BI models.

Table 8.5 Scot Cost of a sample BI model for Scotland in 2020–21

In 2018, mean gross income per head of man, woman and child (Y-BAR) in Scotland was £405.00 pw*. The BIs are set as proportions of Y-BAR, except Pens = Pension Credit.

Pensioner BI (full)	= £173.75 pw	= 0.4300
Working age BI (partial)	= £129.60 pw	= 0.3208
Child BI	= £64.80 pw	= 0.1604
Parent with Care premium	= £32.40 pw	= 0.0802

Col 1	Col 2	Col 3	Col 4 = Col 3 x 365/7	Col 5 = Col 2 x Col 4 div by 1,000
Groups by age or premium	Scot Population 2018 '000s	Sample BI Model, £ pw	Sample BI Model, £ pa	COST of Sample BI Model £m
Whole population	5,438	—	—	—
Pens, 65 +	1,026	173.75	9,060	9,295
Adult 25–64	2,911	129.60	6,758	19,673
Adult 16–24	582	129.60	6,758	3,933
Child 14–15	109	64.80	3,379	368
Child 0–13	810	64.80	3,379	2,737
LoneParent premium	171	32.40	1,689	289
Other PwC premium	383	32.40	1,689	647
To finance the sum of gross transfers, 2020–21			£m	36,942
ADD MARGIN in SCOTLAND for admin costs, HB, DBs etc.			£m	6,750
GRAND TOTAL for all SOCIAL SECURITY 2020–21			£m	43,692

* Rounded up to the nearest multiple of £1.25.

Table 8.5 UK Cost of a sample BI model for the UK in 2020-21

In 2018, mean gross income per head of man woman and child (Y-BAR) in the UK was £472.50 pw*. The BIs are set as proportions of Y-BAR.

Pensioner BI (full)	= £189.00 pw	= 0.4007
Working age BI (partial)	= £151.20 pw	= 0.3205
Child BI	= £75.60 pw	= 0.1603
Parent with Care premium	= £37.80 pw	= 0.0801

Col 1	Col 2	Col 3	Col 4 = Col 3 x365/7	Col 5 = Col 2 x Col 4 div by 1,000
Groups by age or premium	UK Population 2018 '000s	Sample BI Model, £ pw	Sample BI Model, £ pa	COST of Sample BI Model £m
Whole population	66,436	—	—	—
Pens, 65 +	12,166	189.00	9,855	119,896
Adult 25-64	34,505	151.20	7,884	272,037
Adult 16-24	7,141	151.20	7,884	56,300
Child 14-15	1,445	75.60	3,942	5,696
Child 0-13	11,179	75.60	3,942	44,068
LoneParent premium	1,941	37.80	1,971	3,826
Other PwC premium	4,913	37.80	1,971	9,684
To finance the sum of gross transfers, 2020-21			£m	511,507
ADD MARGIN in the UK for admin costs, HB, DBs etc.			£m	82,003
GRAND TOTAL for all SOCIAL SECURITY 2020-21			£m	593,510

* Rounded up to the nearest multiple of £1.25.

Table 8.6 BIs by household type, using the example for Scotland (excludes Housing and Disability Benefits)

Column 1	Col 2	Col 3	Col 4	Col 5	Col 6
£ pw	An income floor:		AHC Poverty Benchmarks		Sample Scot BI Model
Household Configuration		MTBs 2020–21	EU '17–18	MIS 2019	2020–21
Single pens	Pens Cred	173.75	152.08	177.87	173.75
Couple pens		265.20	262.20	279.53	347.50
Single W-A	JSA/ ESA	74.35	152.08	197.71	129.60
Couple W-A		116.80	262.20	335.64	259.20
Young adult, aged 16–24		58.90	152.08/ 110.12	197.87	129.60
Lone Parent + toddler	JSA, CTC, CB	160.13	204.52	288.37	226.80
L Parent + pre + prim-sch		228.35	256.96	367.26	291.60
L P + pre + prim + sec-sch		296.57	367.08	485.71	356.40
Couple + toddler	JSA/ ESA, CTC, CB	202.58	314.64	374.67	356.40
Couple + pre + prim-sch		270.80	367.08	453.11	421.20
Couple + pre + prim + sec		339.02	477.20	581.58	486.00
Couple + all four		407.24	529.64	633.21	550.80

CHAPTER 9
Administrative matters

Co-ordinated or integrated benefit-and-income-tax systems?

IT WOULD HELP THE poorest sections of society if the delivery system for the BIs were to be kept separate from the system for the collection of taxes. The two systems would be *co-ordinated* but not integrated. Taxation at source including the taxation of interest and dividends, and the taxation of employees via PAYE, has the advantage of providing a continuous revenue stream. The collection of taxes on other sources of income could continue to be made after the end of the tax year, as now.

An alternative administrative method has been proposed on occasion, which would only be possible for a BI system that is financed via income tax – the combined Negative Income Tax (NIT) and Tax Credit (TC) method, where the BI and tax systems are *integrated* and net amounts are paid or deducted *in arrears* of the period that it covers. This is a complicated procedure, which involves synchronising information about each worker from three different sources: data from employers about each employee (who could have a portfolio of paid work), and from the relevant administrative bodies such as the HMRC for tax liability and from DWP to calculate a person's benefits. This type of integrated IT system has defeated the UK's new Universal Credit system to date.

Setting up a database

Defining the population and deciding on the eligibility criteria are political decisions. Broadly speaking, administration covers the identification of eligible individuals, assessment and delivery of the BIs and collection of the tax revenues, further monitoring to ensure that individuals continue to fulfil the eligibility criteria, and to effect compliance when they do not. While a BI system decriminalises much of a social security system, the system would need to monitor continually for eligibility, and to check that no one is claiming to be more than one person, nor a parent-with-care claiming for more children than live with her. Biometric records could have an important role to play here. Monitoring also applies to the income tax system, to reduce illegal tax evasion. Nordic-style transparency might help. In some Scandinavian countries, information about the gross income and taxes paid by every individual is available for any other citizen to view online. Many Scandinavians are proud of the amount that they contribute through taxation to a good society.

The first task on implementation would be to set up the database for the BI system. Many citizens are already on one or more databases in the UK. Children receive Child Benefit. Many pensioners receive a state pension or Pension Credit. Many others are already on the Social Security or HMRC databases. The UK Census is an example of a large database, as is the electoral roll which enables a country-wide referendum to be set up at short notice. Many people do not register for the electoral roll, but there would be an incentive to enrol for the receipt of a BI. The existence of these databases should make it easier to set up a new BI database, or to build on a current one.

The numbers will be greater than before, due to the individual replacing the couple as the unit of assessment and delivery and due to universality. For each individual, the database will need to store, among other things, the following information:

- Full name
- Date of Birth
- Gender
- Addresses, current and previous
- Bank Account number
- National Insurance Number
- National Health Service Number
- And links to dependent children, or to the primary care-giving parent or guardian for dependent children.

Some of these items on the database will not change, such as date of birth, or will change only rarely, such as being the primary care-giving parent, or a change of gender. A new birth or a death would have to be notified and recorded. Other changes, such as address or bank account number, could change more frequently.

Delivery

The experience of Child Benefit, which is the closest that the UK has come to granting a universal benefit, provides confidence that a benefit like a Child Benefit for everyone should be relatively easy to deliver.

The BI would be delivered periodically and automatically to those who qualify. Most recent proposals assume that this will be on a monthly basis, in advance of the period to which it applies, but some recipients might find it easier to manage on a fortnightly basis.

To ensure financial autonomy, delivery should be into individual accounts only, not into joint accounts, unless sanctioned by a court of law where an attorney or a *curator bonus* is involved.

Indexation

In order to protect BIs from erosion over time, the level of a BI could be set as a proportion of some measure of prosperity of society, such as gross domestic product (GDP) per head, or mean gross income per head of the population (Y-BAR), and index it for the term of a government administration. This ensures that the scheme remains economically viable. If the economy experiences a downturn, then the BIs in the following year would be less. But this could act as a spur to encourage people to compensate by increasing their work hours and output. Thus, the indexed BIs could help to stabilise the economy.

Implementation

The implementation of a BI system might have some potentially disruptive effects initially. Gradual implementation could minimise this, starting with lower levels of BI, and increasing them by stages to more generous levels over a planned, limited period.

Thus, a *series* of models would have to be designed, with or without a personal income tax allowance, culminating in the aspired-to model. The series will involve increasing the levels of the BIs, particularly for working age adults in the UK, and the relevant tax rates. This will provide the opportunity to correct any initial administrative problems and identify and minimise any adverse unintended consequences. It should allow the population time to adjust to the idea, and to the gradual changes in the tax rates.

If the new BI system were embedded within the current Social Security system, the BIs could be counted as income for assessment for MTBs, reducing the dependence of each claimant on MTBs, but should never leave her with less than she would have been entitled to, prior to the introduction of the BI system. It gives an opportunity to identify anyone who might have become worse off, and to adjust the scheme where necessary. The total expenditure on MTBs will also decrease.

Starting with levels of BI that are so much below the poverty level would prolong the avoidable misery for the most vulnerable. It should be possible to choose a BI model requiring only an income tax rate of 0.32 as the starter model, which is the current standard rate of income tax (20 per cent) that most UK tax payers pay now, plus NI contributions (12 per cent).

An alternative 'sector' approach to implementation, as proposed by Torry (2018: 106), would be feasible, introducing BIs for one demographic group at a time, starting with the most 'deserving' in order to make it more palatable to the general public. However, the corresponding changes in income tax become messy. Are the necessary increases imposed on a sector basis also, such that different rates of taxation apply to different sectors of the population? Or will the whole population be subject to the same increased rate of taxation whether or not they have enjoyed the benefit of the BI? In addition, this process drags out the end goal of a BI for all.

Redeployment of redundant civil servants

If the implementation of the BI scheme requires fewer civil servants to administer it, as anticipated, then potentially redundant civil servants could be offered retraining in areas of their choice, including as income tax inspectors using their experience to increase the pool of people preventing and prosecuting tax evasion. They could also be employed as advisors to low-income people about returning to work, retraining and job opportunities, for instance, and about disability, housing and other retained benefits.

CHAPTER 10

Sources of finance to fund a BI model

Potential sources of finance for a BI model

THE OUTLAY ON THE BI payments can be offset by savings from several sources:

- from the eventual replacement of most NI and means-tested benefits;
- by simplifying the administration of Social Security, thus reducing its costs, and also reducing the risk of fraud and errors by claimants and staff;
- by reducing the costs of poverty alleviation programs after the event and the indirect effects of poverty on the NHS, personal social services and the criminal justice system.

A BI could be financed by a single tax or a combination of taxes. Some people have suggested increases in current taxes, such as VAT and Corporation Tax. Potential reforms of income tax and NI contributions are proposed below.

Some new taxes have been proposed. (A fuller description can be found in Miller, 2017: pp. 163–8.) Their suitability depends on their objectives, propensity to raise revenue and their unintended consequences. The main ones include:

- A *Land Value Tax* (LVT) and other taxes on the ownership of capital; these are effective when the wealth cannot be relocated, such as on land, buildings and other property. It could help to dampen the rise in property prices. The Scottish Greens would like to use an LVT as the basis for a reformed local government tax.

- It is also recognised that if the tax revenue from earnings decreases, then the income derived from capital must be taxed more, but it may require international co-operation to do so.

- A *Sales Tax*, and VAT, are taxes on expenditure. A sales tax of 20 per cent would yield more than VAT of 20 per cent, because VAT paid on goods by VAT-registered businesses can be reclaimed from HMRC. Expenditure taxes tend to be regressive and a dampener on investment and jobs. However, a sales tax, as implemented in many states in the USA, could compensate for this disadvantage by taxing the products sold in the UK of many international companies that currently avoid paying UK Corporation Tax. VAT has been proposed by several advocates as an effective method of financing an EU-wide BI. (See Van Parijs *et al*, 2017: 155-8, 238-41.)

- A *Carbon Tax*, other taxes on pollutants and on the use of scarce resources, are designed to change behaviour, but, when successful, they would reduce the tax base!

- A *Tobin (International) Financial Transactions Tax* on speculation in currencies – requires international co-operation to implement it.

- *Sovereign Wealth Funds* are based on the community control of community-owned natural resources, such as land, water, clean air, minerals, forests, broadcast spectrum, real estate or beaches, which can be used to generate an income. Part of their income could be invested in the international stock market and into alternative social investment projects which could produce a modest income stream. They can help to protect inter-generational equity. These tend to be long-term solutions.

- *Seigniorage*: it has been suggested that BIs could be funded by printing money, as in Quantitative Easing. This would be inflationary in most circumstances, unless the regular injection of money supply is withdrawn equally regularly by some taxation method.

Tax revenues, Social Security expenditure and tax expenditures

So far, recent BI proposals for the UK (as listed in the Select Bibliography below) have concentrated on exploring funding via increases in income tax and NI contributions by employees and self-employed workers, and this well-trod path is followed here. However, it would be relatively easy for a BI scheme to be funded mainly by income tax, but augmented by some other taxes, such as a Land Value Tax, or a Sovereign Wealth Fund (Lansley *et al*, 2019).

Table 10.1 has been abstracted from Appendix A. The three sets of data can be compared as follows.

In 2018, the largest tax yields were from income tax, followed by VAT, then NICs paid by employers, Corporation Tax and NICs paid by employees. These five taxes accounted for nearly £500bn out of a total of nearly £700bn of tax revenue (GCSU).

Total social benefits (NNAD) in each year for 2016–18 were greater than the sum of revenues from household income taxes together with the NICs of self-employed workers and employees. This would imply that income tax and NICs are not necessarily required to finance the other main use of tax revenue, namely, Government Expenditure (spent by Government on behalf of the population on infrastructure and public welfare services). Therefore, increased income tax rates and NICs, if reserved purely for BI payments and associated expenditure, would not be detrimental to these services.

However, NNAD includes 'Other social insurance benefits' (L8R9 + L8RB), which seem to consist mainly of unfunded public-sector pensions, for teachers, NHS staff, firemen, policemen etc. This is not part of the Social Security system.

Deducting (L8R9 + L8RB) from NNAD leaves 'Total Social Security Benefits'. These totals for years 2016–18 barely change, despite the income tax plus NIC totals increasing over the three years, and this latter exceeds the Total Social Security benefits in 2018, by just over £14bn. I assume that this potential shortfall in sources to meet Government Expenditure could be met from elsewhere.

The UK is a medium-taxed country, but is also one of the most unequal nations in the developed world. The current income tax and National Insurance Contribution systems are very unjust and need to be reformed. Both are riddled with tax allowances, reliefs and exemptions that usually favour taxpayers in proportion to their incomes, and they incorporate some underhand methods of favouring the rich.

For example, the Personal Allowance is designed such that when the UK government announced an increase of £500 to £11,500 for the fiscal year 2017–8, it declared that those paying the standard rate of income tax of 20 per cent would be better off by £100 pa. However, it failed to point out that those whose incomes were too low to pay income tax were no better off, while those paying the higher rate of income tax at 40 per cent were better off by £200 pa.

Table 10.1 Tax revenues, Social Security expenditure, and costs of tax expenditures for the UK

REVENUES FROM £m	2016	2017	2018
(DRWH) Household Income Taxes	£172,021	£179,239	£187,022
(NMDE) Self-employed NICs	£3,189	£3,833	£3,691
(GCSE) Employees' NICs	£47,204	£50,483	£52,055
TOTAL	**£222,414**	**£233,555**	**£242,768**
(CEAN) Employers' NICs	£71,407	£76,966	£79,240
(NZGF) VAT	£133,671	£138,922	£149,240
(ACCD) Corporation Tax	£46,708	£56,438	
(CPRO) Corporation Tax			£52,730
Total from all other taxes	£178,261	£186,259	£196,209
(GCSU) Total tax revs – all sources	**£652,461**	**£692,140**	**£720,187**
(YBHA) GDP at current market prices	£1,961,125	£2,040,651	£2,140,278
(GDWM) Total tax yield as % of GDP	33.27%	33.92%	33.64%
(GCSS) Total, all sources → cent G.	£618,279	£656,097	£682,105
SOC. SECURITY TRANSFERS £m	**2016**	**2017**	**2018**
(L8LV) Retirement pensions.	£91,241	£93,212	£96,029
(CSDE) Income Support	£8,108	£7,619	£7,081
(RYCQ) Income Tax Credits & Reliefs	£27,774	£26,268	£23,905
(EKY3) Child Benefit	£11,577	£11,581	£11,374
(EKY5+EKY6) Care and Disability	£21,483	£19,096	£17,829
(CTML+GCSR) Housing benefit	£23,228	£22,052	£20,710
Other social benefits	£39,324	£44,343	£51,663
TOTAL SOCIAL SEC BENEFITS	£222,735	£224,171	£228,591
(L8R9+L8RB) Other social ins bens	£40,826	£41,376	£43,179
(NNAD) TOTAL SOC BENEFITS	**£263,561**	**£265,547**	**£271,770**
COST OF TAX EXPENDITURES £m	**2016–17** *forecast*	**2017–18** *forecast*	**2018–19** *forecast*
National Ins. Primary Threshold	£24,100	£24,900	£26,400
Personal Allowance	£97,400	£101,300	£107,000
Inc tax relief for Regist'd pens schs	£23,850	£24,050	£25,600
Other relief re pension schemes	£20,500	£21,000	£23,300
Other	£72,570	£71,925	£70,450
TOTAL: Income Tax & NIC loopholes	**£238,420**	**£243,175**	**£252,750**

In 2016, the UK government introduced a new method of favouring the wealthy, by setting up a tax-free dividend allowance of £5,000. In the present climate of low returns on investments, anyone who could take full advantage of these exemptions is likely to have a personal financial portfolio of £100,000 or more. However, the dividend allowance was reduced to a mere £2,000 for the 2017–8 fiscal year. Dividends attract a lower rate of income tax than earnings.

The most outrageous pandering to the rich is via the tax reliefs on contributions to registered pensions schemes, worth up to 100 per cent of his/her annual earnings, up to the current annual allowance of £40,000. Tax relief can be claimed at the highest rate of income tax that s/he pays. If someone with an income of £150,000 pa or more puts £40,000 of earnings into one of these schemes, then s/he would receive the full 45 per cent additional income tax relief of £18,000 as a windfall! This concession would be available each year!

One of the reasons put forward for this tax relief is that it provides an incentive for people to save via pension schemes, and saving is important because investment in the private sector is assumed to depend on it. However, the proportion of transactions in the stock market that lead to a genuine increase in expenditure on capital goods for industry is relatively small – less than 7 per cent – the rest merely goes towards a change of ownership of shares. Moreover, the pension schemes are not required to base their pension funds in the UK, so it is not obvious how these schemes contribute to investment in the UK's private sector. The UK economy suffers because so much of home-based saving goes into housing, on account of the quick returns. The UK economy tends to rely on inward investment, when home grown investment would be so much healthier.

New Zealand does not give tax relief on pension contributions, and it provides a contribution-free state pension to anyone who has resided in New Zealand for at least ten years since the age of 20, of which five of those years must have been since the age of 50.

Some tax reliefs are used to encourage outcomes that are in the public interest, such as the work carried out by many charities. Supporting charities through Gift Aid only enhances gifts made by taxpayers rather than by poorer members of the general public. A more efficient method of support would be for the government to give a 25 per cent top up to the donations for every legitimate charity each year. This would be included openly in Government Expenditure accounts, rather than being hidden among the tax loopholes.

The official term for these tax allowances, reliefs and exemptions (and not just in the income tax and NIC systems) is 'Tax expenditures', 'Tax welfare' or 'Fiscal Welfare', since they are equivalent to subsidies, and are an expense to the country (Jones, 2014: chap 6). Just in the income tax and NIC systems alone, they totalled £238bn in 2016–17, and were forecasted to be £243bn and £253bn in the following two years. These tax welfare figures are *even greater* than the expenditure on 'Total Social Security benefits', of £223bn, £224bn, and £229bn in years 2016–18 respectively.

Tax expenditures reduce the tax base and increase the tax burden on those who cannot avoid paying income tax and NI contributions. Rather than being outraged at the size of the Social Security welfare budget, taxpayers and other citizens should be apoplectic at the way and the extent to which wealthy people are subsidised. Rather than favouring wealthy people in proportion to their incomes, as now, it would be much fairer if everyone had a flat rate BI and all paid taxes in proportion to their incomes.

Why income tax is the best source of finance for BIs

All of the recent BI proposals for the UK have relied on changes to the income tax and NIC systems to finance their schemes, and for good reason:

- Income tax is potentially the most direct and efficient system for redistributing income from rich to poor;

- Only income tax and NICs paid by employees and self-employed people could raise sufficient revenue on their own.

- Benefits and income tax are reverse sides of the same coin, both being transfer payments and can be regarded as a single system (even if the two branches are administered separately);

- Similarly, the Social Security budget and the tax welfare system (non-collection of tax revenue through loopholes in the income tax and NIC systems) should be considered as a single welfare system;

- Hypothecating (ring-fencing) the yields from income tax and NIC, to use it solely to finance the BI payments, their administration and related cash transfers (for Housing and Disability Benefits, and other retained benefits), leads to equal upward pressure to increase the level of the BIs and downward pressure to reduce the income tax rate. This imposes a discipline on the system and ensures its economic viability.

- Hypothecating the income tax and NICs separates the system of income redistribution from Government Expenditure. This also implies that all Government Expenditure (on public welfare services and infrastructure, etc) can be financed out of other taxes (and borrowing), as now.

- Procedures are already in place for deducting income tax at source, including from employees' earnings through the PAYE system.

Hypothecation has occasionally been proposed, such as when UK taxpayers expressed themselves willing to pay an extra penny in the £1 of income tax in order to contribute extra funds to the NHS. However, this would cause all sorts of complications. Hypothecation is rarely recommended by economists. However, in this case, its purpose would be to separate the whole system of income redistribution via cash transfer payments from the whole system of Government Expenditure, thus helping to protect each system from encroachment by the other. These are different in principle.

The UK claims to have a system of representative democracy, and yet it is quite clear that none of the major parties has been representing the interests of the poorest and most vulnerable in society over the last four decades. It is also quite clear that governments have tended to make marginal changes in favour of the wealthy whenever possible, and cannot be trusted to treat poorer people fairly. Hypothecation of the redistributive system could make it more transparent and therefore accountable.

The proposed restructured income tax system:

- Merge the current income tax system and NICs paid by employees and self-employed workers into a new income tax system. (No new NI benefit entitlements would be created.)

- Reduce legal tax avoidance by closing most tax loopholes in the current income tax and NIC systems, unless they can be shown to be in the public interest.

> For instance: remove/reduce the Personal Allowance and NI Primary Threshold, since their functions are being fulfilled by the basic income;

> For instance: end tax relief on contributions to registered and other pension schemes.

This will decrease 'tax welfare' and increase the tax base.

- Levy the same rate of the new income tax on all sources of income.

- The structure of the new income tax is either proportionate (a straight-line or flat rate tax), or progressive (with a *maximum* rate for the flat tax, and for the standard rate of the progressive system, of, say, 50 per cent);

- The progressive system could involve:

  a small personal allowance on low incomes;

  the reduction of current, and/or introduction of new, income tax thresholds;

  increasing the current standard rate of income tax;

  higher rates of income tax for all those with higher incomes (*up to* 65 per cent, as already experienced by low-income workers and other claimants via their marginal deduction rates from Universal Credit, and as occurs in some Nordic countries).

- Hypothecate the new income tax system to use it solely to finance the BI payments, their administration costs, and for related cash transfers, such as the separate housing benefit and Disability Benefit systems, and other retained benefits.

- Clamp down on illegal tax evasion.

There is no reason why employers should cease paying NICs, and this now becomes a payroll tax, which could be used to contribute to expenditure on public welfare services.

The BIs and all Disability Benefits will be exempt from taxes on income.

The *gross* cost of a BI scheme is the *sum of gross transfers* – the total amount paid out as BIs to all recipients in a given time period. The *net* cost is defined as the *gross cost minus the savings generated by the BI*, when compared with another BI scheme or some other income maintenance system. See Noguera (2018) for a thought-provoking discussion.

The *sum of net transfers* (for a BI financed by this restructured system) is 'the sum of the amounts of income tax paid, minus the lesser amounts of individual BIs received, by all net income taxpayers' and which is paid to net benefit recipients in the form of transfer payments, that is, the amount of money that 'changes hands'. These two amounts would be equal if there were no administration costs or retained benefits. This measure is 'autonomous', in the sense that it can be calculated without comparison with any other income maintenance system. Nor is it intended as a substitute for the net cost of any BI scheme (as defined above). However, when the sum of net transfers is compared with the sum of gross transfers for that BI scheme, it can be used to gauge *ex post* the distributional impact of the particular BI scheme and its funding method.

A method for costing a BI model financed by a restructured income tax system

Table 10.2 Scot Method for costing a BI model for Scotland in 2020-21

In 2018, mean gross income per head of man, woman and child, Y-BAR, in Scotland was £405.00 pw*. The BIs are set as proportions of Y-BAR, except Pensioner BI = Pension Credit.

Pensioner BI (full)	= £173.75 pw	= 0.4300
Working age BI (partial)	= £129.60 pw	= 0.3208
Child BI	= £64.80 pw	= 0.1604
Parent with Care premium	= £32.40 pw	= 0.0802

Col 1	Col 2	Col 3	Col 4	Col 3 x col 4
Groups by age or premium	Population Scot 2018 '000s	Proportion of population	BI as Proportion of av. inc	Contribution to tax rate
65 or over	1,026	0.18869	0.4300	0.081137
25–64	2,911	0.53531	0.3208	0.171727
16–24	582	0.10692	0.3208	0.034300
14–15	109	0.02007	0.1604	0.003219
0–13	810	0.14901	0.1604	0.023901
All	5,438	1.00000	–	–
PwCs premium	554	0.10187	0.0802	0.008170
To finance the sum of BIs, 2020–21,			t =	0.322454
ADD SCOTLAND's MARGIN for admin, retained benefits, etc t =				0.0587
GRAND TOTAL for all SOCIAL SECURITY,			t =	0.381154
To finance the sum of BIs with EDR,			t =	0.365763
TOTAL INCOME TAX RATE WITH EDR				0.424463
Gross income at which schedules merge, Yo				£76.33 pw
Net income at which schedules merge, Ys				£205.93 pw

* Rounded up to the nearest multiple of £1.25.

Table 10.2 UK Method for costing a BI model
for the UK in 2020-21

In 2018, mean gross income per head of man woman and child, Y-BAR, in the UK was £472.50 pw*.

Pensioner BI (full)	= £189.00 pw	= 0.4007
Working age BI (partial)	= £151.20 pw	= 0.3205
Child BI	= £75.60 pw	= 0.1603
Parent with Care premium	= £37.80 pw	= 0.0801

Col 1	Col 2	Col 3	Col 4	Col 3 x col 4
Groups by age or premium	Population UK 2018 '000s	Proportion of population	BI as Proportion of av. inc	Contribution to tax rate
65 or over	12,166	0.18312	0.4007	0.073376
25–64	34,505	0.51937	0.3205	0.166458
16–24	7,141	0.10749	0.3205	0.034451
14–15	1,445	0.02175	0.1603	0.003487
0–13	11,179	0.16827	0.1603	0.026974
All	66,436	1.00000	–	–
PwCs premium	6,854	0.10332	0.0801	0.008276
To finance the sum of BIs, 2020–21, t =				0.313022
ADD UK's MARGIN for admin, retained benefits, etc t =				0.0502
GRAND TOTAL for all SOCIAL SECURITY, t =				0.363222
To finance the sum of BIs with EDR, t =				0.355001
TOTAL INCOME TAX RATE WITH EDR				0.405201
Gross income at which schedules merge, Yo				£93.29 pw
Net income at which schedules merge, Ys				£244.49 pw

* Rounded up to the nearest multiple of £1.25.

Tables 8.5 above costed a sample BI model in terms of £bn. Tables 10.2 for Scotland and for the UK, provide an easier and more informative method of costing the same sample BI model, but in terms of the required income tax rate from the restructured income tax system described above.

- Column 2 records the population in each age group.
- The proportion of the total population represented by each age group is noted in column 3.
- The amounts of the BIs are expressed as proportions of the latest available value for Y-BAR (the mean gross income per head of man, woman and child, rounded up to the nearest multiple of £1.25), and noted in column 4.
- The product of columns 3 and 4 is recorded in column 5, which gives the contribution of each group to the cost in terms of the income tax rate required.
- The amounts are summed over the groups. This gives the total flat rate of (restructured) income tax required to finance the sum of gross transfers of the BI model.

A margin (as described in chapter 8, Table 8.4) must be added to the sum of gross transfers to cover administration costs, and the costs of retained benefits. The grand total gives the flat rate income tax required to finance the whole Social Security system.

The reason why the method is based on funding a BI model with a *proportionate* (flat rate) income tax is that it is much easier to calculate. The calculation based on funding by a progressive income tax would require information on the distribution of the incomes of *all individuals*, and the UK government does not collect these on a comprehensive basis. Information about the distribution of the income of individual taxpayers is collected, but that only covers 46 or 47 per cent of the population, or 57 or 58 per cent of the adult population in the UK. Information on the poorer half of the population is collected only on a household basis and is published annually in the DWP's *Households Below Average Income*. But household figures mask potential inequality within the household. The flat rate calculation provides a single cost figure by which to summarise and compare each BI model.

Parallel income tax schedules – an earnings or income disregard

Since this type of BI model grants different levels of BI to working age people and pensioners, for instance, all of whom pay the same rate of income tax, then it will lead to parallel income tax schedules, when net income is plotted against gross income. While differences in BI might be justified for people when their gross incomes are zero, it is harder to justify that same difference in net incomes associated with a higher gross income. This can be avoided by introducing an *earnings or income disregard* (EDR) for those receiving the lower BI, such that they pay no tax on their first tranche of gross income until their income tax schedule meets and merges with that of people receiving the higher BI. The government foregoes the tax revenue on that first tranche. The reduced tax revenue would have to be compensated for by slightly increased tax rates for the resultant income tax schedule.

Fortunately, both the new tax rate and the point at which the schedules merge are easy to calculate. It can be shown that this adjustment will cost no more (and is likely to be less) than if those receiving the lower BI and eligible for the disregard had received the higher BI instead. This new rate of income tax, t, to finance the new sum of gross BI transfers (ie excluding the added margin) can easily be obtained using the method in Tables 10.2 above.

Then, the gross income, Yo, at which the two schedules merge, is given simply by:

$$Y_o = (\text{higher BI} - \text{lower BI}) / t.$$

The net income, Ys, at which the two BI schedules merge, is given by:

$$\begin{aligned} Y_s &= \text{lower BI} + Y_o \\ &= (\text{higher BI} - (1 - t).\text{lower BI}) / t. \end{aligned}$$

CHAPTER 11

Who says we can't afford an adequate BI system?

THIS CHAPTER IS DEVOTED to providing methods for:

- calculating the cost of lost income tax revenue as a result of creating a small personal allowance;

- providing a quick method for calculating the cost of a BI scheme with a full BI for all adults, and

- working out where the break-even point occurs between a proposed BI scheme and the current UK income tax schedule.

How much would a small Personal Allowance cost in terms of lost income tax revenue?

The BI itself serves the same function as a Personal Income Tax Allowance (PITA). But, if there were no PITA, then everyone would have to pay tax on their first £1 of earned or other gross income. This could increase the number of tax returns that HMRC would have to process. There would be advantages to both citizen and HMRC if a tax return did not have to be completed where it concerns only casual earnings of say £40 pw (£2,080 pa), or £60 pw (£3,120 pa), or children's pocket money. In this case, a small PITA can be built into the BI scheme. The government foregoes tax revenue when the PITA is implemented, but, again, the reduced tax revenue would have to be compensated for by slightly increased income tax rates. The untaxed tranche of income would provide an increased incentive to work-for-pay, even if only part-time.

It is difficult to make an accurate estimate of the cost of a PITA without accurate information about the distribution of gross incomes at the lower end of the range. How many adults have a gross income of less than £3,120 a year, for instance?

It was reported in chapter 2 that in the UK in 2018 there were at least 7.049 million working age people who were 'economically inactive'. If we assume that they and 1.38m unemployed people had a gross income of £0 (before benefits or tax), then a total of 8.429 million had no gross income of their own. Thus, in a graph of the distribution of gross incomes of individual adults in the UK, there would be a spike at £0 of 8.429m and the other 45.383m adults will have had some positive gross income (based on *Blue Book* estimates, see Appendix A below).

We still do not know the distribution of individuals' gross incomes between £0 and £3,120. To obtain an extremely cautious estimate, it is safer to assume that all of the other 45.383 million adults had an income of at least £3,120, which would have been taxed if there had been no PITA. Let this number of adults be represented by N. If a PITA of £3,120 is then created, it will cost the exchequer, in terms of revenue foregone, a further (£3,120 x 45.383m x t) = £141.595 x t bn, where t was the straight-line income tax rate required to finance the sum of the BIs for the particular BI model. This estimate is likely to fall, if actual numbers of individuals on low incomes became available.

In the sample model used in Table 10.2 UK, t = 0.3130. Thus, revenue foregone will be £141.595 x 0.3130 = £44.319bn. Dividing this by the total income for the UK (£1,634.013bn) gives 0.0271, which is the increase in tax rate required from 0.3130 to 0.3401. Adding on the cost of the margin (0.0502) gives a grand total of 0.3903 after introducing the PITA of £3,120 into that particular model.

To summarise, the increase in the income tax rate required to finance a small PITA is given by:

PITA x N x t / Total Income.

Approximate cost of a model with the same full BI for all adults

While the examples given in Tables 10.2 above are useful to demonstrate how the costing method works, it is even easier to obtain a ballpark figure for the cost of the same full BI for all adults. The population of adults in both the UK and Scotland is just over 80 per cent and so that of children is just under 20 per cent. This gives an easy way to anticipate the cost of a model where these are the only two age groups. The approximate cost for the alternative AHC poverty benchmark proposed in chapter 8, where the full BI for all adults is 0.4 of Y-BAR, and that for children is 0.2, is as shown in Table 11.1.

Table 11.1 A method for estimating the approximate cost of models that give full BIs to all adults

Age group	Proportion of population	BI as proportion of Y-BAR	Contribution to t
Adult, 16+	0.80	0.40	0.32
Child, 0-15	0.20	0.20	+0.04
Cost of BIs			=0.36
Margin			+0.05
Total			=0.41

The required tax rate for this scheme over the years will remain roughly the same as long as the demographic profile stays roughly the same.

Adding a small PITA of £3,120 in 2020–21 would increase the cost of the scheme by £3,120 x 45.383m x 0.36 = £50.974bn for the UK scheme. This, divided by total income £1,634.013bn, increases the tax rate by 0.0312 to 0.3912. Adding on the cost of the margin, as above, yields 0.4412.

Thus, even this more generous BI scheme with a tax-free PITA, if paid for by an otherwise straight-line income tax, would not cost more than t = 0.44 or 0.45. This is still below my self-imposed constraint of t = 0.50, and is less than the UK's current highest rate of income-tax-plus-NICs of 0.47. This in itself could pose a dilemma, whether to allow those on the highest incomes to profit from the introduction of a BI scheme, or levy higher rates of income tax on higher levels of income.

How to calculate the breakeven points between a BI model and the current income tax schedule

Without access to an appropriate computer-based tax-benefit microsimulation model, it is impossible to analyse the distributional impacts of this proposed BI scheme. However, the following analysis tries to give an idea of some of the gainers and losers from the implementation of the BI system.

In the following two Tables 11.2 for 2020–21:

- Column 1 gives the current tax schedule for the income of a working age person; for incomes above the Upper Earnings Level (UEL = £962pw x 52 = £50,024 pa), NICs are reduced to 2 per cent

- Column 2 gives the current tax schedule for the income of a pensioner, who is not subject to NICs;

- Column 3 gives the tax schedule for a working age adult receiving a partial BI of 0.32 of Y-BAR, and subject to the relevant income tax rate calculated for 2020-21 data via the method as indicated in Tables 10.2, but with a higher rate of income tax, 0.50, imposed on higher incomes in order to create a breakeven point when compared with column 1.

- Column 4 gives the tax schedule for all adults, receiving a full BI of 0.40 of Y-BAR, and subject to the relevant income tax rate calculated for 2020-21 data via the method as indicated in Tables 10.2, and increased as a result of a personal allowance of £3,120 pa (to 0.47 for Scotland and 0.45 for the UK), but with a higher rate of income tax, 0.50, imposed on incomes greater than £50,000 in order to create a breakeven point when compared with column 1.

Pensioners in Scotland would receive the greater amount of £173.75 pw in order not to be worse off than under Pension Credit.

Figure 11.1 presents the information provided in Table 11.2 UK in visual form, comparing the two BI models with the two 2020–21 income tax schedules. It illustrates the significant increase for low-income individuals, and shows that the advantage for working age individuals decreases as can be seen for gross incomes greater than £20,000. From an income of about £50,000, the BI schedules and the current income tax schedule are more or less co-incidental, with relatively small differences. However, the differences are more marked for pensioners.

To find the break-even level of gross income, Y_g, between a current tax schedule and a BI model, one must identify the section where the breakeven takes place. For the examples given for working age adults in Table 11.2 UK (comparing

Table 11.2 UK Tax schedules, UK, 2020–21

	Col 1	Col 2	Col 3	Col 4
	Current schedules		**BI models**	
Gross Income, Y_g	*NIC* t Y_n	t Y_n	t Y_n	t Y_n
£0	£0	£0	£7,884	£9,855
	0.00 / 0.00	0.00	0.37	0.00
£3,120	£3,120	£3,120	£9,850	£12,975
	0.00 / 0.00	0.00	0.37	0.45
£9,516	£9,516	£9,516	£13,879	£16,493
	0.12 / 0.00	0.00	0.37	0.45
£12,500	£12,142	**£12,500**	**£15,759**	**£18,134**
	0.12 / 0.20	0.20	0.37	0.45
£50,000	£37,642	£42,500	£39,384	£38,759
	0.12 / 0.40	0.40	0.50	0.50
£50,024	**£37,653**	£42,514	**£39,396**	**£38,771**
	0.02 / 0.40	0.40	0.50	0.50
£100,000	£66,639	£72,500	£64,384	£63,759
	0.02 / 0.20 / 0.40	0.20 / 0.40	0.50	0.50
£125,000	£76,139	£82,500	£76,884	£76,259
	0.02 / 0.40	0.40	0.50	0.50
£150,000	£90,639	£97,500	£89,384	£88,759
	0.02 / 0.45	0.45	0.50	0.50
£200,000	£117,139	£125,000	£114,384	£113,759

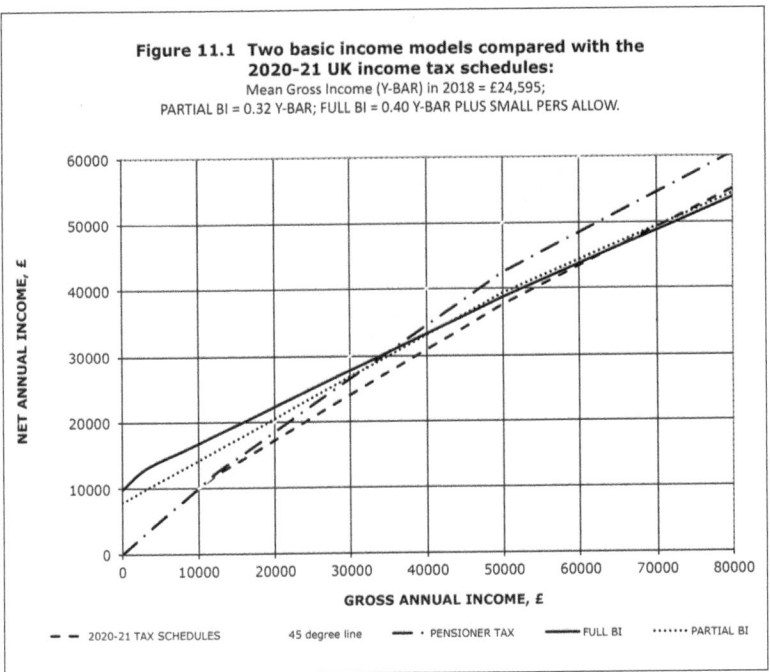

Figure 11.1 Two basic income models compared with the 2020-21 UK income tax schedules:
Mean Gross Income (Y-BAR) in 2018 = £24,595;
PARTIAL BI = 0.32 Y-BAR; FULL BI = 0.40 Y-BAR PLUS SMALL PERS ALLOW.

column 1 with either col 3 or col 4), Yg occurs in the current UK higher income tax range. However, pensioners get a very good 'NIC = 0' deal, and so their breakeven point occurs in the lower, standard rate of income tax range.

The breakeven level of Yg occurs where the net incomes, Yn, are equal.

Thus, comparing column 1 and column 4,

Yn in column 1 is 37,653 + (1 − 0.42).(Yg − 50,024), and
Yn in column 4 is 38,771 + (1 − 0.50).(Yg − 50,024).

Equating these two expressions leads to:

$$0.08 \times (Yg - 50,024) = 1,118$$
$$Yg = 50,024 + 1,118 / 0.08$$
$$Yg = 63,999.$$

PART III – PRACTICAL ISSUES: DESIGNING AND COSTING A BASIC INCOME MODEL

That is, the breakeven point between column 1 and column 4 occurs at Yg = 63,999. The breakeven point between column 1 and column 3 occurs at Yg = 71,812. Further breakeven points occur below and above Yg = 125,000.

For pensioners, the breakeven point between column 2 and column 4 occurs at Yg = 35,036.

However, in column 3, the pensioner will be receiving the full BI of £9,855 pa, rather than the partial BI of £7,884 pa, so the pensioner schedule is greater by £1,971 pa.

Thus, comparing columns 2 and 3, the pensioners' breakeven point occurs at Yg, where:

Yn in column 2 is $12,500 + (1 - 0.20).(Yg - 12,500)$, and
Yn in column 3 is $15,759 + 1,971 + (1 - 0.37).(Yg - 12,500)$.

Equating these two expressions leads to:

$0.17 \times (Yg - 12,500) = 3,259 + 1,971$
$Yg = 12,500 + 5,230 / 0.17$
$Yg = 43,265$.

Table 11.3 UK Summary of the gross incomes at the breakeven points in Table 11.2 UK

2020–21		Tax schedules, UK	
Yg at breakeven points		**Working-age, Col 1**	**Pensioners Col 2**
Working age, partial BI	Col 3	£71,812	
Working age, full BI	Col 4	£63,999	
Pensioner's = partial BI + £1,971	Col 3		£43,265
Pensioner, full BI	Col 4		£35,036

There could be some advantage in implementing a new scheme over a planned limited period, such as the five years of a government administration, with the first stage introduced in year 1, the second in year 3 and the final stage in year 5. If tax expenditures were removed by year 1, the stages for the BI scheme in Table 11.2 column 4 could be implemented as shown in Table 11.4 UK (based on data for 2020–21).

The standard rate of tax required for the first stage would be no more than that paid by working age people in the UK in 2020–21 (0.20 income tax plus 0.12 NICs). That of the aspired-to, most generous BI model, implemented by year 5, is less than the income tax and NIC rates for even the highest-taxed individuals in the UK, and there would have been no breakeven point if a higher rate of income tax of 0.50 had not been introduced for incomes greater than £50,000. This breakeven point is as high as £64,000. Thus, a large proportion of the adult population could be better off financially as a result of its introduction, while working age individuals with gross incomes of £200,000 would only be £3,000 or £4,000 worse off than under the 2020–21 UK tax regime. However, the real losses are those sustained by people whose tax expenditure privileges have been removed, and a micro-simulation model would be needed to estimate the distribution of these.

Table 11.4 UK Gradual implementation of proposed alternative poverty benchmark BI

UK £ pw	Year 1	Year 3	Year 5
Groups by age or premium			
65+	189.00	189.00	189.00
16–64	94.50	141.75	189.00
0–15	94.50	94.50	94.50
PwC	47.25	47.25	0.00
t			
Tax rate	0.2474	0.3102	0.3626
PA, £3120	0.0208	0.0260	0.0305
Margin	0.0502	0.0502	0.0502
Total tax rate	0.3184	0.3864	0.4433

The comparable results for Scotland are as follows.

Table 11.2 Scot Tax schedules, Scotland, 2020–21

	Col 1	Col 2	Col 3	Col 4
	Current schedules		**BI models**	
Gross Income, Y_g	*NIC* t Y_n	t Y_n	t Y_n	t Y_n
£0	£0	£0	£6,758	£8,447
	0.00 0.00	0.00	0.38	0.00
£3,120	£3,120	£3,120	£8,692	£11,567
	0.00 0.00	0.00	0.38	0.47
£9,516	£9,516	£9,516	£12,658	£14,957
	0.12 0.00	0.00	0.38	0.47
£12,500	£12,142	£12,500	£14,508	£16,538

	Col 1	Col 2	Col 3	Col 4
	\multicolumn{2}{c}{Current schedules}	\multicolumn{2}{c}{BI models}
Gross Income, Y_g	*NIC* t Y_n	t Y_n	t Y_n	t Y_n
	0.12 0.19	0.19	0.38	0.47
£14,585	£13,581	£14,189	£15,801	£17,643
	0.12 0.20	0.20	0.38	0.47
£25,158	£20,771	**£22,647**	**£22,356**	**£23,247**
	0.12 0.21	0.21	0.38	0.47
£43,430	£33,013	£37,082	£33,685	£32,931
	0.12 0.41	0.41	0.38	0.47
£50,000	£36,101	£40,958	£37,758	£36,413
	0.12 0.41	0.41	0.50	0.50
£50,024	**£36,112**	£40,972	**£37,770**	**£36,425**
	0.02 0.41	0.41	0.50	0.50
£100,000	£64,598	£70,458	£62,758	£61,413
	0.02 0.205 0.41	0.205 0.41	0.50	0.50
£125,000	£73,723	£80,083	£75,258	£73,913
	0.02 0.41	0.41	0.50	0.50
£150,000	£87,973	£94,833	£87,758	£86,413
	0.02 0.46	0.46	0.50	0.50
£200,000	£113,973	£121,833	£112,758	£111,413

The breakeven points for the 2020-21 Scottish income tax and BI schedules were calculated in the same way as for the UK schedules. If pensioners received the full BI of at least £162 pw in column 3, it would add £1,689 to their net incomes. However, if Scottish pensioners are not to be worse off under the BI scheme, then they must receive at least the same as Pension Credit, £173.75 pw, which adds another £613 pa. The results are recorded in Table 11.3 Scot.

Table 11.3 Scot Summary of the gross incomes at the breakeven points in Table 11.2 Scot

2020-21		Tax schedules, Scotland	
Yg at breakeven points		Working-age, Col 1	Pensioners Col 2
Working age, partial BI	Col 3	£73,107	
Working age, full BI	Col 4	£54,495	
Pensioner's partial BI + £1,689 + £613	Col 3		£36,987
Pensioner, full BI + £613	Col 4		£32,293

Again, the proposed BI scheme in column 4 could be implemented over a five-year period, with the tax rates as indicated in Table 11.4 Scot.

The third stage in year 5 would require a tax rate of 0.47, which is less than the 2020-21 Scottish additional tax rate of 0.46 together with NICs of 0.02. A higher rate of income tax of 0.50 on incomes over £50,000 creates a breakeven point. All working age taxpayers with an income of less than £54,000 could be better off financially, and individuals with incomes of £200,000 would only be two or three thousand pounds worse off.

Table 11.4 Scot Gradual implementation of proposed alternative poverty benchmark BI

Scotland £ pw	Year 1	Year 3	Year 5
Groups by age or premium			
65+	173.75	173.75	173.75
16–64	81.00	121.50	162.00
0–15	81.00	81.00	81.00
PwC	40.50	40.50	0.00
t			
Tax rate	0.2540	0.3184	0.3725
PA	0.0254	0.0318	0.0372
Margin	0.0587	0.0587	0.0587
Total	0.3381	0.4089	0.4685

Clearly, it is possible to devise an economically viable, adequate BI model for the UK, or for a fully-fiscally devolved Scotland, funded by a restructured income tax system with a standard rate of income tax that is less than the 2020–21 additional rate of income tax plus NICs for those with the highest incomes.

This could be politically achievable if future governments no longer made marginal changes in favour of the wealthy. Instead of giving them tax breaks in proportion to their incomes, the government should share the combined Social Security welfare and tax welfare budgets equally among the population of the country.

PART IV

Where next?

CHAPTER 12

Economic effects of BI

Work incentive effects and labour supply

SOME CRITICS CLAIM that if people had an adequate, unconditional BI, they might give up paid work. However, all of the evidence shows that people want paid employment.

Economic theory recognises two incentives that influence the number of hours in a given period that a worker wishes to offer in any particular job (her/his labour supply). An increase in unearned income, such as from the introduction of a BI, is expected to have a small negative effect on the labour hours, except for those who are deprived of leisure or income, who have more elastic labour supply curves. The other incentive is the real net wage rate that they face, after the deduction of income tax, NICs and benefit withdrawal tapers.

A decrease in the net wage rate, due to an increase in the income tax rate, could have either a negative or positive effect, and thus could either further decrease the hours of work offered or offset the negative effect, partially or fully.

In contrast, for low-waged workers and other claimants, the fall in the rate of marginal deductions from earnings, and hence an increase in the net wage rate, resulting from the ending of means-testing for most benefits, could have a positive effect on their very elastic labour supply curves, and thus the labour hours offered. The resultant increase in the net wage rate could raise it above the reservation wage, below which workers are unwilling to offer their labour in a particular type of work. Thus, there could be an increase in the number of low paid workers who formerly were unemployed or 'economically inactive'.

Apart from the numbers in the labour force, their conditions of work could be considerably enhanced by a BI system. The financial security of the BI could reduce the chronic stress arising from the uncertainly of the gig economy. Unconditionality, backed up by financial security, could reduce the inequality of power relationships in the workplace. It could enable workers and their representatives to negotiate co-operatively for reasonable pay and good working conditions, or to refuse the worst jobs, depending on the employment situation and whether there were other job opportunities. Thus, it could enhance industrial democracy. Wage rates for unpleasant drudge jobs are likely to rise, unless they can be automated, while those of comfortable, interesting, pleasant work could fall. A BI system could work well for either a full employment economy or one affected by further job losses.

Poverty-prevention levels of BI (rather than income-replacement for the main earner) would provide financial security for more people, offer them more control over the use of their own time, give them more choice and flexibility in life, helping them to develop to their full potentials. The more generous the BI, the greater the effects, which could help to lead to a culture of joyful work, both paid and unpaid.

Basic income and the British Trades Unions

British Trades Unions have been latecomers to the BI debate. Their National Welfare Charter was first launched at a fringe meeting of the TUC Congress in September 2015, supported by the UNITE union among others, which called for

> 7. An end to the sanctions regime and Work Capability Assessment – full maintenance for both the unemployed and underemployed. We need a non-

> means-tested, non-discriminatory benefit payable to all, with housing costs met allied with extensive provision of low-cost housing.

It continues:

> Achieving dignity, independent living and the ability to participate in society must be cornerstones of our Social Security system. We must explore ways of achieving this such as growing the numbers of people who support the principle of a minimum Citizen's Income for all. (Welfare Charter, 2015)

At the TUC Congress in September 2016, a shortened version of the Welfare Charter was passed, proposed by the Trades Union Councils.

Also at the TUC Congress 2016, UNITE proposed, and USDAW seconded, a motion containing the following section:

> Congress notes the growing popularity of the idea of a 'Universal Basic Income' with a variety of models being discussed here and around the world.
>
> Congress believes that the TUC should acknowledge Universal Basic Income and argue for a progressive system that would be easier to administer, easier for people to navigate, paid individually and that is complementary to comprehensive public services and childcare provision.
>
> The transition from our current system to any new system that incorporates these principles should always leave people with lower incomes better off. (TUC, 2016: 27)

On the whole, those TUs that represent low-paid workers can see that their members are likely to benefit from the introduction of a BI. Higher paid workers probably benefit as much as anyone from the current system, although a BI would give more financial security, especially with the anticipated changes in employment due to technological change and further automation. Some union officials may worry that BIs might reduce the power and influence of the unions themselves.

The business case for BI

At the end of chapter 3, the effects that a BI could have on the lives of individuals were noted, including emancipation through more control over the use of their own time, together with financial security and claimants facing lower marginal deduction rates from their earnings. It is assumed here that the BIs will be financed via a restructured progressive income tax system, as discussed in chapters 10 and 11, and that the BI systems will be implemented gradually over a planned limited period, accompanied by the closing of tax loopholes and increasing income tax rates.

Now it is time to see things from the point of view of employers and businesses. Everyone, employers and employees alike, will have an unconditional BI. The effects on the world of business will depend on the level of the BI, the attitudes of employers, the skill levels of different groups of workers, and the demand for labour, which determines whether workers have many alternative job opportunities.

Certainly, the initial levels of the BI, during a gradual implementation, would not be enough to live on and enable workers to walk away from their jobs if they were dissatisfied. Wage protection will still be required, and preferably trades unions would be able to work in their members' interests more freely than in recent times, as unions do in the Nordic countries. As the level of the BI increases towards a full BI during the implementation period, the level of the Living Wage Foundation's Living Wage (which estimates the wage rate necessary to provide a worker with enough to live on, including rent or mortgage interest, travel-to-work costs and the extra costs incurred when working), could fall gradually.

Means-tested in-work benefits provide an incentive for employers to reduce their workers' wages, whose losses will be partially compensated for by the MTBs. This has the effect of subsidising employers. The difference with BI is that the level of the BI remains the same and is independent of the income of the worker. Thus, there is less incentive for employers to exploit their workers in this way.

But, employers might find that a falling National Living Wage (NLW) over time entitles them to reduce their workers' wage rates (or at least not to increase them as much), and they might expect to increase their profits. However, the same will be happening to all of their competitors, and competition should compete away any excess profits. If the NLW does fall over time, and the prices of their products also fall, then companies could become more competitive in world markets, competing against low-wage economies, and increasing their exports. UK workers would be assured of enough to live on and the choice of walking away from wage rates that are below their reservation wage threshold, or from poor working conditions.

The implementation of BIs is likely to regenerate areas of multiple deprivation. The well-being of the residents should improve, and there will be a general increase in demand for products and services. New companies will want to move into the area, investing in the local economy and workforce. Some residents with renewed confidence may turn their hand to starting their own local businesses.

Self-employed people, small businesses and workers' co-operatives often find it difficult to obtain loans from banks or other financial institutions, which would enable them to invest in their own companies. A BI could provide that financial security which would allow them to invest and grow. Financial security not only reduces stress and anxiety, but it releases creative forces.

It is anticipated that the BIs will help to reduce material poverty and improve the well-being of the population, in terms of security, health and education opportunities. A healthy workforce is an asset, reducing the number of days lost from absenteeism.

Given this situation, would profitable firms want to relocate from Scotland to England – in the case of a BI system being implemented in Scotland first – or from the UK to other countries? If the BI system is financed from income tax, and taxes on corporations are not increased, there is no obvious incentive to relocate profitable businesses.

Macroeconomic effects of BI

The main questions about the effects of a BI scheme on the macro-economy concern its likely effects on GDP. If the financing of the BI scheme is purely by redistribution of incomes through taxation, then the deadweight loss (any reduction) to the economy should be negligible. While the introduction of a new system might bring about some temporary disruption, these are likely to be minimal if the scheme is implemented gradually. The larger concern is not proven. Why would replacing the current social security system with an unconditional BI scheme necessarily lead to slower growth?

Assuming that the levels of the BIs are indexed to a lagged value of mean income per head (as illustrated in PART III above), then if falls in GDP and total income were to occur, it would lead to a fall in BIs during the following fiscal year. Assuming that an increase in unearned income in the form of a BI will reduce labour hours, then conversely, a reduction in the BI should increase them, by incentivising people to increase their labour hours to make up the difference. This should allow the indexed BI to act as a self-stabilising mechanism and also fiscal drag could reduce the amplitude of economic cycles.

The implementation of BIs financed by a progressive income tax system should help to redistribute incomes, effectively ending austerity, which has had such a negative effect on the UK economy and delayed its recovery by some years. Redistribution of income will certainly give a boost to the national economy, since poor people tend to consume a larger proportion of their incomes than wealthier people, who save more and spend more on luxury imports. The national economy provides a stable basis for exports.

A second concern is whether the introduction of a BI scheme would be inflationary. If the BI system is financed out of taxation, then a BI system merely transfers money from one part of the economy to another. If no new money is being introduced into the economy, then the BI scheme is not expected to be inflationary. However, if the supply of certain goods does not expand to meet demand, then price rises could be expected. The inadequate supply and distribution of affordable housing could be a particular concern. However, this is still a problem caused by housing policy, and cannot be expected to be solved by the income maintenance system.

The big unknown about the future of either the Scottish or UK economies is the effect of further automation. Technical change in the past has led to the creation of new jobs, but the big questions now are 'how many?' and 'what sort?'

Even with increased automation, demand for labour is likely to be secure for the foreseeable future, in skilled, high-salaried, innovative jobs in these and other hi-tech industries. It should also be secure in the creative industries, the caring professions and personal services where the personal touch is important, such as in the complementary therapies for example. Growth industries are likely to include education, health maintenance and leisure.

But automation has already encroached on many unskilled jobs, and is now affecting employment based on access to information. 'Precarity' has even reached the professions, including academia, the law and accounting. It will take longer, if ever, to replace a whole range of practical jobs such as plumbers and electricians, police, fire and rescue services. There could be a risk of creating further income inequalities, splitting the working population into high and low wage earners. Education could be the long-term solution here. It is clear that the world of work is undergoing a revolution and the underlying assumptions and institutions that regulated it for the past seven decades may no longer apply. The automation revolution could hasten the introduction of a shorter standard working week.

The other effect of the continuing trend towards automation, is its shift away from labour income to income from investment in new technology and capital equipment. Every effort must be made to ensure that this source of income is taxed, either through corporation tax, and as one of the components of personal income that is subject to income tax. International co-operation will be required to tax income from capital. If this fails, then a Sales Tax could recoup a share of the profits going to capital and contribute to the financing of the BI system.

Automation, both past and future, will probably have a far larger impact on our lives than the implementation of BIs, but a BI system is more likely to help us weather these unknown changes than the present broken UK Social Security system.

But the government will have to play its part, too. Markets should be regulated for the health and safety of both consumers and workers. They should also be regulated to prevent monopolies and oligopolies from forming and exploiting consumers and workers. The government could support the economy by investing in infrastructure (for passenger and freight transport, communications, broadband development, etc). It should also invest in human capital, through education and skills-training programmes, to improve productivity. However, the other factor for improving productivity is investment in capital goods. Home-grown, as well as inward, investment should be encouraged.

The government should also take measures to *improve* other areas such as health services and social care, childcare services, services for people with disabilities, the supply of social and other affordable housing, and also policies for wealth redistribution here in the UK, one of the most unequal countries in the developed world.

CHAPTER 13

The anatomy of basic income pilot experiments

Microsimulation models and pilot experiments.

COMPUTER-BASED TAX-BENEFIT microsimulation models and BI pilot experiments are research tools that serve different purposes, and each can contribute to our knowledge about the effects of the introduction of a BI scheme. Each is a method of generating data which can be collated, transferred to data files and subsequently interrogated using standard statistical and other techniques. Each can be used to examine the effects of fiscal changes – of a variety of different types of benefits (contributory, means-tested and universal), and of NI contributions and various tax regimes.

Each method has its strengths and limitations. The microsimulation model can be used relatively cheaply to explore distributions of net incomes, to estimate numbers still in poverty and calculate inequality indicators. BI pilot experiments take longer and are much more expensive, but they can analyse the likely behavioural and attitudinal effects of BI schemes.

Each method starts with a sample of subjects who are surveyed. The microsimulation might have access to an anonymised sample from the Family Resources Survey (formerly the Family Expenditure Survey), while the pilot experiment selects its own sample.

Each sample survey will typically provide standard demographic data and social characteristics, including date of birth; gender; kinship and other household relationships; living standards; health status; disability status; highest educational level attained so far; and, for adults, work status, and housing tenure.

In addition, it will include financial information about assets, wage rates, sources of gross income, net income after current benefits have been added and tax deducted, patterns of expenditure, savings and debt. Also, information will be noted about the number of hours per week spent in employment or other work-for-pay, travel to work, caring for children or others, in addition to personal maintenance, domestic chores, and leisure pursuits.

The strength of a microsimulation model lies in its ability to calculate the net incomes of individuals or households resulting from a variety of different benefit and taxation regimes, based on their initial gross incomes. The net incomes, or the differences in net incomes resulting from different fiscal regimes, can then be plotted against gross income. The microsimulation model can be used to compare the resulting net incomes against poverty benchmarks, to estimate how many people or households would still be in poverty. It can be used to identify groups of gainers and losers and also to measure the inequality of the distribution of net incomes.

Some microsimulation models may estimate the likely *change in working hours* resulting from the changes in benefits and taxes, based on theories and assumptions about labour supply behaviour. Other models are static, in that the number of working hours carried out by an individual is assumed to remain the same, regardless of changes in financial incentives. Microsimulation models are unable to gauge either behavioural or attitudinal effects of different regimes, and this is their major shortcoming.

Thus, they are unable to gauge the emancipatory effects of the tax and benefit changes, or the effects on people's use of their own time, interactive effects in a community, macroeconomic effects, or the effects of either a long-term or a lifetime BI. But it has no ethical implications, because its results do not affect real people, as long as the original survey data are anonymised. Obviously, ethical concerns could arise when applying the results in real-life policies.

Although microsimulation software takes time and skill to develop, once created, it is much cheaper to use compared with the cost of a pilot experiment, and many different output files can be created for further analysis. The software would have to be updated regularly to adapt to a country's current benefit and taxation schedules. Each microsimulation model is only as good as the assumptions on which it is based.

The strength of a pilot experiment is that it can analyse the *behavioural* and *attitudinal* effects of a BI. Its baseline survey at the start of the project could obtain far more information about each sample subject's living conditions, food and nutrition, tobacco and alcohol consumption, illness and use of healthcare services, current schooling, further and higher education and skills-training, together with other uses of their time, in addition to that of working-for-pay and caring. The repetition of the survey at regular intervals enables both the major life changes in the household (marriage or divorce, a death or a new baby), in health (accidents, physical and mental illnesses or recoveries), in educational status, at work (redundancy, promotion, a new job), or in housing, to be recorded, as well as changes in the uses of time.

Basic income pilot experiments have limitations:

- Neither a random sample nor a saturation sample can be absolutely universal, since it necessarily excludes those outside the sample.

- If participation in a pilot experiment were voluntary, the sample certainly would not be representative of the whole country. Wealthy individuals are more likely to be underrepresented, since a BI system could leave them worse off financially, and they would be more likely to opt out. If participation were mandatory, it would have to have official backing and presumably, in this case, wealthy individuals could be made worse off.

- However, even some mandatory basic income pilot experiments impose the condition that no one (not just poor people, but rich ones too), should be made worse off financially by participating in the experiment, a condition known as 'no detriment'. Thus, the pilot would not be able to assess the likely behavioural effects of a BI scheme on wealthier individuals if it were to be implemented nationally, with clawback through the tax system. In this situation, if the BI scheme were financed by income tax, the basic income would be effectively zero for sample subjects with higher levels of income. Thus, the ability of experiments to explore the redistribution effects of BIs and their sources of funding is limited.

- Pilot experiments cannot pick up macroeconomic effects, for instance, on demand for labour, changes in productivity, wages and prices, average profit rates for businesses, new companies moving into deprived areas, new investment in the local economy and workforce. A large saturation sample should be able to pick up some of these effects at the local level.

- Pilot experiments are at risk of being curtailed mid term, by the election of a new government, for instance, as occurred in Ontario in 2018.
- The short duration of most such projects – typically 24 ± 12 months – enables some short-term effects to be detected, but not long run ones, nor those of a lifetime basic income.

Neither microsimulation analysis, nor BI pilot experiments, can provide evidence of long-term effects of a BI system.

Basic income pilot experiments raise some **ethical** issues:

- Some people claim that giving different levels of BI in an experiment is treating human beings as 'lab-rats', and that the project should provide only the most generous BI level possible. However, if this latter proposal were rolled out nationally, it could have a very disruptive effect on the economy and compromise the other possible good effects of the system. It is essential to learn what the effects of different levels of BI could be and how long those effects might take to become manifest.
- Those outside the BI experiment are excluded – thus, some citizens could benefit from the expected advantages of the BI experiment, but not others.
- At the end of the BI experiment, subjects should be supported (through their BIs being reduced gradually over time to the current benefit levels), and their earlier rights preserved, when they return to their previous social security situation.

BI pilot experiments

BI pilot experiments require time, expertise, resources and commitment. Those involved in running the project must be committed for the long haul.

A pilot experiment can have several objectives:

- educational – to inform members of the public about the desirability and feasibility of BI, and to encourage them to engage with their elected representatives on the subject, so that these latter will be well-educated and positive about it when the time comes for votes to move it on to its subsequent phases.

- to test hypotheses about the *behavioural* effects of different levels of BI and different types and levels of financing.

- to test hypotheses about the impact of BIs on *attitudes*.

- to demonstrate its administrative and economic viability in practice.

Typically, a BI pilot experiment would follow several distinct stages:

- Planning could take 2–3 years, and should include:

  - the design of the experiment, including that of the actual BI models to be used;

  - an estimation of the costs, and exploration of financial sources to fund the BI, preferably securing the whole budget in advance;

  - In addition, a public education program (conducted by voluntary organisations) is essential, to help to inform the population, and to persuade them to engage with their elected representatives.

- The implementation phase would probably last a further 2 or 3 years, and there could be advantages for it to coincide with the fiscal year (6 April to 5 April the following year in the UK).
- The evaluation stage comprises collation and analysis of the data generated.
- Finally, the dissemination of the results, to officials, media and the public, in the form of reports, articles and events.

The planning stage

This is the most important phase, where thorough preparatory work is essential, and it should not be rushed. This phase determines whether one has a well-designed experiment or ends up with a set of data which is unable to yield answers to the questions posed.

A core multi-disciplinary research team would work closely together to plan and design the actual basic income experiment. When necessary, opinions could be sought from specialist advisors, including a statistician specialising in experimental design, a social security expert, an economist and a psychologist, among others.

The key to any experiment is the identification and formulation of the questions for which answers are sought and their specification as hypotheses that can be tested empirically, which will determine the information that is collected. These will include general questions about BIs, such as, might there be significant differences in the effects of a BI between urban and rural areas, or how long does it take for the main effects of BI systems to be fully manifest, in addition to specific questions about the effects of individual models.

Three main areas must be designed for the experiment:

- The actual basic income models implemented – the levels of BI that are paid to the sample subjects, together with the method of financing the models.

- Sample sizes and methods: how subjects are selected for the treatment and control groups, allowing for 'wastage' through relocation or death.

- The baseline questionnaire that is to be put to the sample subjects and control groups, to elicit the relevant data for analysis. Also, the questions to be put to other agencies to obtain further information.

Thus, the core team would explore with the public and others in the host areas, what questions they want to be asked as part of the experiment and what outcomes they want the BI models to achieve. They might want to find out whether subjects prefer a BI rather than a means-tested benefit of the same amount. However, is gaining an answer to this last question worth the cost to the sample subjects of being kept on the same below-poverty levels of BIs as the means-tested benefits for all or part of the duration of the experiment?

The team would devise the appropriate models involving different levels of basic income. Each level of basic income would have associated with it a corresponding rate of income (or other) tax, which could be levied until the basic income effectively became zero (or negative if wealthy individuals were allowed to become worse off). The varying levels of basic income can be implemented at different times or to different samples, to test many aspects of basic income models, gaining maximum information, while avoiding unnecessary repetition. The models should also specify whether and how existing means-tested Social Assistance benefits are to be treated. Existing National

Insurance benefits would not normally be affected for an experiment, even though many could be replaced by a BI in a nationally implemented scheme.

The core team would advise on the size of, and sampling method for, the treatment and control groups, to ensure that the analysis is statistically rigorous. Samples for an authentic basic income pilot experiment should cover all income groups. Eligibility criteria will have to be established for inclusion in the project (and for retention, if re-location occurs during the implementation stage). Typically, no new subjects would be added, except for new spouses and new babies.

A saturation sample of people in a defined geographical area enables the impact on the local community to be assessed, but it is unlikely to be a representative sample of the whole country, which would require random sampling. A random sample could be stratified, that is, augmented with extra subjects from smaller groups who are under-represented in the population, and who could be the focus for some special questions (such as care-leavers, or lone parents, for instance). Others who are recognised as at risk include disabled people, single low-skilled working age males, those with high debt levels and those facing high rents. In a random sample, an individual could be the only person in a family or household receiving a BI, and the outcomes might be different from the situation where all members of the family are recipients. Ideally both saturation and stratified random samples would be used.

The team would design the baseline questionnaire, to be completed by the treatment and control groups initially for a baseline survey, and repeated at regular intervals, and this should ensure that the information collected will enable the appropriate hypotheses to be tested. Some of the information that could be collected in the baseline questionnaire was noted above. The questionnaire would be pre-piloted, that is, tested on some individuals or villages which would not be selected later as a treatment or control group.

The team would advise on the different types and frequency of intervention that would be required. In addition to the baseline questionnaire, for instance, other surveys, diaries, case studies, or the use of other sources, such as administrative registers, could be useful.

An experiment may involve several host areas with different interests and priorities. If one host area wants to ask specific questions of a particular group of the population in its sample area, then that question should appear in the baseline questionnaire, so that all of the other host areas would also ask the same questions of that group in their sample areas, to maintain as large a sample size for that group as possible.

The amount of relevant information that can be generated by the experiment should be maximised, to create a database that can be analysed over future years. The marginal cost of the research program is a relatively minor part of the whole project, compared with the major cost of the outlay on the basic incomes.

Unless it is a privately-financed initiative, the team would also have to engage with national and local governments, benefit agencies and revenue administrations, to obtain any necessary support. The team could also contact researchers who have made use of relevant microsimulation models, and also those in other countries who have set up basic income, or other similar types of, experiments, to learn from their experiences.

They would learn that the context in which each pilot experiment takes place could help to prioritise its objectives in terms of perceived problems, such as poverty and inequality, or labour market difficulties. If the effects of BI on community are sought, then these take longer to manifest, affecting the duration of the experiment and also indicating the use of saturation samples.

Context can also impose constraints. The prospect of forthcoming elections can affect the timing and duration of an experiment, as in Finland and Ontario. Other constraints include the need for a change in legislation, attitudes to non-conditionality, and cost limits.

The need for early planning for each stage of the pilot – development, design, implementation, evaluation and dissemination – would be emphasised. Similarly, the importance of rich qualitative data from which to draw narratives and stories of participants' personal experiences, and of regular communications about its aims, status and reporting schedule throughout the project would also be pointed out (Barclay *et al*, 2019).

Towards the end of the planning phase, the complete proposal would have to be put to the relevant authorities, for approval to progress it to the implementation phase.

The implementation stage

Once the BI experiment has been given the go-ahead, the samples will have to be selected. An awareness day of public meetings would inform the public about the aims of the pilot project.

The treatment groups must be prepared for their roles, which could involve setting up new bank accounts. (BIs should not be paid into joint accounts.) A delivery system for the planned BI models will have to be in place.

The main activity will be the interventions for gathering data, from both treatment and control groups. Teams of field numerators, recruited and trained to conduct the interviews, would help the treatment and control group subjects to complete the questionnaires. Interventions comparable to the ones carried out in the Indian BI pilot experiment (Davala et al, 2015: chapter 2) could include the following:

- A community survey before the start and at the end of the pilot study would collect information about the socio-economic structures of the villages used in the saturation samples, including pupils' ease of access to primary and secondary schools, public transport services, proximities to medical practices, pharmacies and hospitals, etc.

- The baseline survey at the very beginning of the project could be completed by the same subjects and members of the control groups at six-monthly intervals and continue until its end, producing a panel survey. For a duration of two years, there would be five surveys, and for three years, there would be seven. In the Indian context, there were three – a baseline census, an interim survey halfway through and a final evaluation survey at the end.

- A post-final evaluation could be made some months after the end of the pilot to explore the lasting effects of the experiment, and subsequent attitudes to it.

- The survey data could be supplemented by a further set of family case studies of households, and specialist information could be collected from designated key informants, such as doctors and teachers, about the effects on their communities.

- Administrators could be asked about the differences that they experienced in delivering the BI compared with the previous and subsequent MTBs. Social workers could be questioned as to whether their clients experienced less stressful and more confident lives. Employers could be questioned as to their experiences in, and attitudes as a result of, the experiment.

Later stages

The data collected via the surveys would have to be collated and transferred to data files, ready for analysis using standard statistical and other methods.

The results of the analyses would be written up for the different audiences – the technical experts, the politicians and the general public – using a variety of media, the printed word, the spoken word and presentations around the country.

The costs of a basic income pilot project

The costs of a basic income pilot experiment can be divided into two parts:

I. The costs of implementing the experimental basic income models, with different levels of basic income, would probably fall to official sources:

- The cost of the basic income models, including the sum of the gross transfers (total cost of the basic incomes paid to the sample subjects for the duration of the project), constitutes by far the major part of the expenditure for the experiment. However, savings from floating subjects off SA benefits, lower administration costs, and the revenue from the chosen system of funding, means that the final cost of the experiment would be less than this.

- The salaries and expenses of the basic income delivery and tax-collecting team(s);

- The salaries and expenses of the team that would ordinarily support the sample subjects to adjust to changes.

II. The extra costs of conducting a multi-disciplinary research program could be met by official sources, matched by grants from grant-awarding bodies;

- The salaries and pension contributions of the core research team for the planning phase, the duration of the experiment, and the analysis and dissemination periods.
- Other expenses: equipment and software, travel costs, salaries of field enumerator staff, dissemination costs, etc.

The anticipated savings and potential sources of finance are as listed in chapter 10. If official bodies are not involved in the delivery of the BIs, then the savings from displaced benefits may not be repatriated to the BI-awarding body, but at least they can be estimated. (On a more limited scale, an increased Child Benefit could simulate a Child BI for those families with dependent children in the UK, because this is not taken into account when families are assessed for MTBs.)

The reduced cost of administering the BI scheme can be calculated and compared with that of the current system.

The potential savings from improved health outcomes can also be estimated from changes in the number of General Practitioner and hospital visits, and in the number of prescriptions. Similarly, changes in crime levels in the saturation sample areas could be gauged.

If the official bodies are not involved in helping to administer the experiment, then it would be difficult to levy the tax changes associated with different BI models. However, it might be possible to deliver a pre-taxed BI, where the BI is delivered net of the income tax rate associated with a given model, based on total earnings and other gross income received during the previous tax year, using tax codes issued by the tax collection agency. This method could also simulate a smaller Personal Allowance, and even new income tax thresholds, if required by the financing method. If no one is allowed to become worse off, then where the net amount would have become negative, the sample subject receives zero. Closing tax loopholes, introducing new taxes or clamping down on illegal tax evasion would be outwith the competence of a team in the UK without the co-operation of HMRC.

Certainly, a well-planned pilot experiment could provide answers to many questions, give the administrative authorities the opportunity to iron out practical problems, and also create a major data bank, a resource that would be of interest to researchers around the world for years to come.

CHAPTER 14

Conclusion

The nature of criticism of BI

IF SOMEONE EXPRESSES an opinion that they prefer society as it is, compared with the vision offered here, then that is not a criticism of the vision. If someone prefers apples to pears, that is not necessarily a criticism of pears. Similarly, criticisms of a particular model may be justified, but they cannot be taken as criticisms of the generic concept.

So, what constitutes valid criticism, and what is merely a difference in preferences? In chapter 3, I listed some common objections to the defining characteristics of BI, noting which are 'normative' (value-based) and which are 'positive', that could be tested empirically. BI is an instrument. Both the broad outcomes claimed for it, and the mechanisms identified as the means by which they are brought about, could be questioned. For instance, will the uniformity of a BI really make the effective income tax rates on earnings less regressive, compared with MTB's, and help to reduce income inequalities? Alternatively, proof that *exactly the same outcome*s could be achieved more efficiently or effectively by some other method would be valid criticism.

It is certainly true that many UK taxpayers are completely unaware of the acute misery that is meted out to millions of claimants and low-paid workers on a daily basis. They don't see any need for a reform at all, or they claim that increased benefit levels and a few tweaks at the margins would solve the problem of poverty, for instance, without understanding the structural flaws in the current system that would prevent this from being achieved. It certainly behoves critics to address these structural flaws, or justify them if they can. Some of the most vociferous critics seem to be equally ignorant of the growing BI literature, and appear not to have done any homework before firing off their comments, and adding confusion to a debate that can already be complex and technical.

Some critics claim that most people in Britain think that income should be related to work, as in earnings. But does that include all income – or what about interest and dividends or rental income? Does it include all work? What about currently unpaid work?

The most frequent objection to BI schemes is that they will 'cost too much', but no one seems prepared to say how much is 'too much'. How rich does a country have to be before it feels that it can take care of, let alone invest in, its poorest and most vulnerable citizens? If the anticipated outcomes are valued highly, a BI scheme, even if costly, could still be good value for money. The examples given in chapters 10 and 11 demonstrate that adequate BIs models can be designed and financed by a fairer restructured income tax system, which still leaves the majority of the population as gainers financially. Some may baulk at increased income tax rates, but if it is accompanied by an increase in net income for the majority, why would people object? If someone were offered one millions pounds sterling, on condition that they would pay a 50 per cent income tax on all future sources of income, would they reject the deal? Nevertheless, controlling the cost of a BI system is an important objective.

Some people worry that rich people would emigrate if personal income taxes rise, taking their profitable companies with them. Yet employees of international companies enjoy working in Nordic countries, in spite of their high rates of income tax. Other things, such as political stability, security, cultural diversity, a temperate climate and the English language are often even more important.

Others worry about the effect of a change to a BI system on the economy. Some are concerned in case it decreases demand, others that it will increase it, at a time when developed nations should be reducing material consumption and carbon footprints.

Some who like the idea of BI in principle still harbour doubts. Many of the reservations of critics are political, in the sense that they fear that the alliances that have been forged over decades to protect the interests of certain groups in society (trades unions, for instance) could be undermined. Others worry about the practicalities of implementing a BI system, mainly on account of its interaction with the current complex NI system and Social Assistance safety net.

Others are sceptical that any proposed BI scheme will ever be successfully implemented, since they fear that it is likely to be sabotaged by powerful political forces before completion. Even worse, a BI system could be in place, with the current Social Security system more or less dismantled, and then a new government might scrap it altogether, or more likely, redefine it and use it for their own different purposes. Certainly, constitutional safeguards would have to be in place to protect against such an event, and to protect the BI levels from erosion. Other legal protection is also required to protect one's BI from debt-collection, and to make it illegal for an individual to use his/her BI as security for a loan or a mortgage, which, if it went wrong, would deprive the individual of his/her future income stream and put her/him at risk of permanent destitution.

Alternatively, several rich industrialists have backed the idea, but people are distrustful of their motives, especially when some of the billionaires want to use a BI system as an excuse to replace all public welfare services in addition to their Social Security systems. And yet, the undermining of our public welfare services has been happening already in the UK, under recent governments. We need to reclaim our democracy, and fight for both a BI system and our welfare services. Some people advocate Universal Basic Services (UBS). These are not alternatives to a BI, otherwise how would food and clothing be distributed, to say nothing of housing and utilities? BI and UBS are complements. We need both. I would prioritise BI in order to prevent poverty. UBS would make other necessities available that are better provided for as public services.

Some people like the idea of a BI, but worry about whether the anticipated good outcomes will actually manifest, or whether there will be adverse unintended consequences, which they are not willing to risk.

The political process

Although the idea of BI has been around for a long time, interest has increased markedly in recent years. There could be several reasons for this – the continuing adverse effects of the financial crisis of 2008, and of climate change. Globalisation has hit unskilled, low-waged people particularly hard. The widening inequality in both income and wealth is becoming more evident. The UK Social Security system has been undermined over recent decades and it is failing to tackle poverty, financial insecurity and increasing personal debt. It is estimated that 20 per cent of the UK population is now living in poverty, which adversely affects the life-chances of children. The failings of the Social Security system are becoming hard even for the public to ignore. But the final straw is the perceived potential threat of further massive unemployment from new technologies and automation in industry.

The Westminster political parties are very aware that the current UK Social Security system is well past its sell-by date, but none of them – except for the Green Party of England and Wales – appears to be prepared to stick its neck out and promote a radical alternative to the existing flawed system, unless it has first been made safe to do so. 'Safety' comprises two aspects.

First, some BI advocates believe that there is already enough evidence available about the potential outcomes of BI systems in general, and that a BI pilot project would just be a delaying tactic. Others are in favour of a BI experiment, because it will provide recent evidence in the context of a western nation with a well-developed Social Security system. Even more importantly, it could check for any adverse unintended consequences. In the UK, Child Benefit was introduced without testing it, and it is a great success, even though its values have been eroded over time. On the other hand, Universal Credit has been rolled out without a proper experiment, and it has been a disaster. Governments want to look as though they are making evidence-based decisions.

So, a demonstration of the practical viability of a BI system is necessary to show that even a relatively generous BI scheme is *economically viable*, that setting it up and its gradual implementation can be administered competently and that it will not have a disastrous effect on the economy; furthermore, that it will deliver the expected short-term and long-run advantages, even in the face of possible behavioural changes in line with the incentive effects. The Scottish BI feasibility study could demonstrate some of these, if it is progressed to implementation.

The community of BI advocates is multi-disciplinary, and over the years has provided a grounding of theoretical research covering a range of topics, analysing BI in different contexts: BI with respect to different ideologies, to work incentives and the labour market, to trades unions, to women, to people with disabilities, to ecology, alternative currencies, a world-wide BI, to political strategies, and to theoretical aspects of BI experiments. This is now being followed by more empirical experimentation and computer-based microsimulation analysis, mapping the topics in the theoretical foundation. More is needed. There is room for constitutional experts and lawyers to propose the safeguards that will be needed, and for sociologists and psychologists who could establish the necessary conditions for a compassionate, stable, sharing community. Would a BI be a necessary condition and what other criteria are needed? An exploration of more progressive income tax schedules and other sources of funding, either on their own or in combination, to finance BI schemes, would be welcome. Also, how much does poverty and insecurity cost the NHS and other key public services, and so what might be the savings from a BI system that reduced poverty and insecurity?

Secondly, *political achievability* will be based on a widespread education program leading to broad social acceptance by both the grassroots and the political classes, and all becoming familiar with the concept, its definition, desirability, feasibility, the criticisms made against it, together with the counter arguments. The early stages of the debate have been based on the theoretical academic research, backed up by empirical results. Now, for dissemination to occur, the conversation must change from academic discussion to techniques for framing the ideas, using narratives and stories, in ways that are easy to understand. The academic and activist communities are complementary and must work co-operatively to influence the public, opinion-formers, policy-makers and politicians.

Members of the public would be encouraged to engage with their elected representatives, to ensure that they, too, are fully briefed and aware of their constituents' views on the subject. A coalition of advocates would be very helpful.

In other words, a well-informed public must clamour for it and thoroughly-briefed politicians must be able to speak in favour of it with confidence. Two educational charities, the Citizen's Basic Income Trust and the more recently formed Citizen's Basic Income Network Scotland, along with their partner organisations, have important roles to play. Training workshops for *cognoscenti* who would be willing to write and speak as ambassadors at public meetings could be an important way forward. The converts will be mobilised to convince the electorate, who will convince the politicians. Conferences and debates will also help the public to clarify their own ideas.

How might the BI model to be implemented be chosen?

Let us look further ahead to a time when an All Party Parliamentary Group agrees that a BI system would be the best way forward and a Parliament is ready to introduce a Basic Income Bill. To what BI model might they aspire, after the initial phase of implementing entry-level schemes? Three possibilities could be considered:

- Each political party would include details of its favoured model in its manifesto for the next General Election or Scottish Election, and the party that is elected must implement its model, or a coalition would negotiate a compromise between their two models. If the amounts in the scheme to be implemented were indexed by being expressed as a proportion of mean gross income per head of the population, Y-BAR, then the scheme could be adopted for the five-year administration period of the government, thus reflecting the prosperity of society. The shortcoming of this method is the potential volatility of the proposed basic income schemes of the political parties every five years, undermining the aim of increasing financial stability, especially for the most vulnerable.

- It would be preferable if an All Party Parliamentary Group could agree to adopt a poverty benchmark. There are three candidates:

    1 the EU/UK official poverty benchmark,

    2 the more generous alternative BI poverty benchmark proposed in chapter 8 and explored in chapter 11, or

    3 the even more generous one presented by the Minimum Income Standards group.

- The last suggestion is that the working age population could be invited to vote for the flat-rate income tax in a restructured income tax system that they would be prepared to pay to fund a BI model. This would be conditional on all of the tax raised being ring-fenced to be used for a BI scheme, while being aware that an extra 0.05 or 0.06 would have to be added to cover the margin of costs of administration and retained benefits. For instance, if the mean of the tax rates for which the population voted turned out to be 30 per cent, then it could be used for a working-age BI of 0.30 of Y-BAR. Slightly more could be allocated to pensioners and parents with care, and slightly less for children, but the actual income tax that would be levied would be approximately 30 + 6 = 36 per cent.

Hope for the future

The world is facing the prospect of major crises ahead. The worst and most urgent of these is the environmental one comprising population growth, profligate consumption, resource depletion, pollution of all types, especially plastics, the increase in greenhouse gases leading to climate change, loss of species, all caused by ignorance, negligence and the casual degradation of our beautiful planet.

While globalisation has led to an increase in material standards of living on average around the world, it has increased the dominance and profits of large corporations, while undermining the wage rates and living standards of low and unskilled workers. Technical change, artificial intelligence and automation have had similar effects. Poverty and increasing inequality are still major problems.

A BI system has great potential at a global level. An international BI scheme could have an important role, helping to invest in the people of poorer nations, giving them the opportunity to develop creative lives for themselves in their own countries and cultures, as demonstrated in the experiments in Namibia and India. It could help to reduce the instability caused by mass migrations of people across the world. Thus, while a BI could help directly in tackling poverty and inequality, it would not necessarily tackle the major environmental problems directly, but maybe it could act as an enabler, taking the strain off ordinary humans and giving them the time and resources to tackle the environmental problems.

The UK and its constituent nations now face a time of great flux. The Referendum on 23 June 2016 on whether to remain in or leave the EU has led to a vote for Brexit, and, in the process, has revealed the enormous divisions in prosperity in UK society. Rather than being about the EU, the referendum was more likely to have been about the voters being fed up with the Establishment and wanting to give it a bloody nose, for looking after its own interests while neglecting those of weaker sections of the population. A generous BI might have avoided the chaos that has ensued, and will be even more necessary after Brexit.

The neoliberal policies over four decades in the UK have led to increasing inequality, contributed towards the financial crisis of 2008 and to the recession that followed. The subsequent austerity programmes have hit the poorest sections of society hardest and delayed economic recovery. Cuts in welfare benefits have increased financial insecurity and personal debt. The labour market has been changing quickly, not only for low-waged and unskilled workers in insecure, part-time jobs, but the professional classes are also being affected. The resultant stress is one of the factors that has led to an increase in demand for health services. A BI scheme could help to increase financial security and reverse the trend towards greater inequality in the UK.

One purpose of this book has been to demonstrate that changing the characteristics of current social assistance systems into those defining a BI can enable it to fulfil a set of broad objectives based on compassion and justice. These would underpin the type of society that many people would like to create for themselves and future generations.

A second purpose has been to show that economically viable BI schemes can be devised to meet the poverty benchmarks put forward by reputable institutions, if governments would only refrain from favouring the wealthier sections of society in proportion to their incomes through tax breaks, and distribute a basic amount to everyone instead.

The key to a politically expedient BI system is:
- to provide adequate BIs that could meet the needs of most individuals and reduce inequality, and
- to control costs to affordable, sustainable levels, while retaining incentives to work for pay.

If the BI scheme is financed by a progressive income tax system, then it is merely transferring income from rich to poor people, and will not be a dead weight loss on the economy, and the distribution effects are far more important than the overall cost. Why would the majority of the people object to higher income tax rates, if it would make them better off? Affordability is not necessarily about low levels of taxation, but value for money for the outcomes achieved.

Another purpose has been to encourage people to inform themselves about BI and discuss it with family and friends and within their other spheres of influence. Governments are more likely to listen to a groundswell of informed opinion demanding a change to this new system, than to a few disparate voices.

There will be times of great uncertainty ahead, to which has been added that associated with the onset of the coronavirus pandemic. However, Covid-19 has provided the strongest case yet for the immediate introduction of a permanent or temporary basic income both in the UK and world-wide. A basic income is not a sufficient condition on its own for a better society, but it is a necessary one. It could bring out the best in people, and change our society from one of fear and despair into one of compassion, justice, trust and hope. It would be an important development towards the new relationships between society, the state and its citizens here in the UK, in other countries, and on a global scale for world justice. It could help to transform societies into ones where everyone matters and all can flourish. At home, it could lead to a new Scottish Renaissance.

Appendices

APPENDIX A

Data for the UK and Scotland, 2016–18

Table A.1 Figures for the UK, 2016–18

UK	2016	2017	2018
POPULATION: total	65,648,054	66,040,229	66,435,550
aged 65 or over	11,814,085	11,989,322	12,165,557
aged 0–15 inclusive	12,390,097	12,505,357	12,624,179
POPN: ECONOMICALLY ACTIVE / INACTIVE, Aged 16+			
(MGRN) Employees	26,760,000	27,068,000	27,494,000
(MGRQ) Self-employed	4,766,000	4,794,000	4,780,000
(MGSC) Unemployed	1,633,000	1,480,000	1,380,000
(MGSF) *Economically active	33,360,000	33,536,000	33,819,000
(MGSI) Economically inactive	19,090,000	19,241,000	19,215,000
(MGSL) TOTAL	52,450,000	52,777,000	53,034,000
(YBHA) **GDP** at curr mkt prices, £m	1,961,125	2,040,651	2,140,278
GDP per person: £ per annum	£29,873.00	£30,900.00	£32,216.00
(IHXT) £ per week	572.91	592.60	617.84
(QWMF) **INCOME** £m	1,500,403	1,531,004	1,634,013
Mean gross Income per head £ pa	£22,855.25	£23,182.90	£24,595.46
(Y-BAR) £ per week	438.32	444.60	471.69
BASIC INCOME – EXAMPLES	**2018–19**	**2019–20**	**2020–21**
Pension or full BI £ pa	£9,142.10	£9,273.19	£9,838.18
= 0.40 of Y-BAR: £ pw	176.00	178.00	189.00
Partial BI = 0.32 of Y-BAR: £ pa	£7,313.68	£7,418.55	£7,870.55
for adults (aged 16–64) £ pw	140.80	142.40	151.20
SOC. SECURITY TRANSFERS £m	**2016**	**2017**	**2018**
(L8LV) Retirement pensions £m	£91,241	£93,212	£96,029
(CSDE) Income Support	£8,108	£7,619	£7,081
(RYCQ) Inc Tax Credits and Reliefs	£27,774	£26,268	£23,905
(EKY3) Child Benefit	£11,577	£11,581	£11,374
(EKY5+EKY6) Care and Disability	£21,483	£19,096	£17,829
(CTML+GCSR) Housing benefit	£23,228	£22,052	£20,710
Other social benefits	£39,324	£44,343	£51,663
TOTAL SOC SEC BENEFITS	£222,735	£224,171	£228,591

UK	2016	2017	2018
(L8R9+L8RB) Other soc ins bens	£40,826	£41,376	£43,179
(NNAD) **TOTAL SOC BENEFITS**	£263,561	£265,547	£271,770
COST OF TAX EXPENDITURES, £m	2016–17 forecast	2017–18 forecast	2018–19 forecast
National Ins. Primary Threshold	£24,100	£24,900	£26,400
Personal Allowance	£97,400	£101,300	£107,000
Inc tax relief for Regist'd pens sch	£23,850	£24,050	£25,600
Other relief re pension schemes	£20,500	£21,000	£23,300
Other	£72,570	£71,925	£70,450
Total: Income Tax & NIC loopholes	£238,420	£243,175	£252,750
REVENUES FROM: £m	2016	2017	2018
(DRWH) Household Income Taxes	£172,021	£179,239	£187,022
(NMDE) Self-employed NICs	£3,189	£3,833	£3,691
(GCSE) Employees' NICs	£47,204	£50,483	£52,055
(CEAN) Employers' NICs	£71,407	£76,966	£79,240
(NZGF) VAT	£133,671	£138,922	£149,240
(ACCD) / Corporation Tax (CPRO) Corporation Tax	£46,708	£56,438	£52,730
Total from all other taxes	£178,261	£186,259	£196,209
(GCSU) Total tax revs – all sources	£652,461	£692,140	£720,187
(GCSS) Total, all sources → cent G	£618,279	£656,097	£682,105
NUMBERS OF TAXPAYERS / NON-TAXPAYERS '000s	2016–17 forecast	2017–18 forecast	2018–19 foreccast
Non-taxpayers 0–15	12,390	12,505	12,624
16–64	17,444	17,046	17,046
65 +	5,424	5,729	5,796
TOTAL	35,258	35,280	35,466
Income taxpayers 16–64	24,000	24,500	24,600
65+	6,390	6,260	6,370
(All) TOTAL	30,400	30,800	30,970
Of which, taxpayers: at highest rate	4,340	4,260	4,280
at additional rate of income tax	330	368	393

UK			
NAT INS AND MEANS-TESTED BENEFIT RATES £ pw	2018–19	2019–20	2020–21
State Retirement Pension, single	£125.95	£129.20	£134.25
New State Pension, single	£164.35	£168.60	£175.20
Pension Credit, single (w/d 40%) couple	£163.00 £248.80	£167.25 £255.25	£173.75 £265.20
JSA/ESA Single person, aged 25+ Couple	£73.10 £114.85	£73.10 £114.85	£74.35 £116.80
JSA/ESA Single person (16–24)	£57.90	£57.90	£58.90
***Universal Credit single, 25+ (paid calendar couple, 25+ -monthly) 1st child (w/d 65/63%) subsequent children	£317.82 £498.89 £277.08 £231.67	£317.82 £498.89 £277.08 £231.67	£323.22 £507.37 £281.25 £235.83
Incapacity Benefit – long-term: – short-term (under pension age)	£109.60 £82.65	£112.25 £84.65	£144.15 £86.10

Personal Independence Payment:
Daily Living Component – enhanced
                                      – standard
Mobility Component   – enhanced
                                      – standard
	
	£85.60
	£57.30
	£59.75
	£22.65
		
		£87.65
		£58.70
		£61.20
		£23.20
			
			£89.15
			£59.70
			£62.25
			£23.60

Carer's Allowance	£64.60	£66.15	£67.25
Child Tax Credit, 1st child (w/d 41%) subsequent children	£63.77 £53.32	£63.77 £53.32	£64.73 £54.27
Child Benefit: 1st child subsequent children	£20.70 £13.70	£20.70 £13.70	£21.05 £13.95
Nat. Minimum Wage, 25+, £ ph	£7.83	£8.21	£8.72
Living Wage Foundation, 18+, £ ph	£9.00	£9.30	
NET DISPOSABLE EQUIVALISED HSHLD INCOMES – COUPLES	2015–16 £ pw	2016–17 £ pw	2017–18 £ pw
Mean (BHC)	593	594	613
Pov benchmk, 1st adult is 0.5 x 0.67	199	199	205
Mean (AHC)	516	517	536
Pov benchmk, 1st adult is 0.5 x 0.58	150	150	155
Median (BHC)	481	494	507
Pov benchmk, 1st adult is 0.6 x 0.67	193	199	204
Median (AHC)	413	425	437
Pov benchmk, 1st adult is 0.6 x 0.58	144	148	152

* These *Blue Book* and HMRC figures do not add up.

** Recipients of Means-Tested Benefits are usually eligible for Housing Benefit and Council Tax Benefit/Reduction also.

*** Universal Credit is paid each calendar month in arrears.

The weekly amount can be calculated as follows:

weekly amount = monthly amount x 12 / 365 x 7.

Universal Credit (UC) replaces six benefits: Income Support, Jobseeker's Allowance, Employment and Support Allowance, Child Tax Credit, Working Tax Credit and Housing Benefit. UC gives weekly figures very close to JSA amounts.

Table A.2 Figures for Scotland, 2016–18

SCOTLAND		2016	2017	2018
POPULATION: total		5,404,700	5,424,800	5,438,100
aged 65 or over		998,852	1,012,567	1,026,114
aged 0-15 inclusive		915,917	917,442	919,502
GDP current mkt prices,	£m	148,295	155,191	163,576
GDP per person: £ per annum		£27,438.00	£28,608.00	£30,079.62
£ per week		526.21	548.64	576.86
INCOME	£m	113,990	114,303	114,568
Mean Income per cap	£ pa	£21,090.90	£21,070.45	£21,067.65
(Y-BAR)	£ pw	404.48	404.09	404.04
BASIC INCOMES – EXAMPLES		**2018–19**	**2019–20**	**2020–21**
Pension or full BI	£ pa	£8,439.36	£8,428.18	£8,427.06
= 0.4 of Y-BAR:	£ pw	162.00	162.00	162.00
Partial BI (for adults),	£ pa	£6,749.08	£6,742.54	£6,741.65
= 0.32 of Y-BAR:	£ pw	129.60	129.60	129.60

See the Main Sources of Data below.

APPENDIX B

WORK BOOK: Design and cost your own BI model

Photocopy, or use pencil for, these tables.

Table B.1 Scot Costing a BI model in £m for Scotland, 2020–21

Col 1	Col 2	Col 3	Col 4 = Col 3 x365/7	Col 5 = Col 2 x Col 4 div by 1,000
Groups by age or premium	Scot Population 2018 '000s	Your own BI Model, £ pw	Your own BI Model, £ pa	COST of your own BI Model £m
Whole population	5,438	—	—	—
Pensioner, 65 or over	1,026			
Working-age, 25–64	2,911			
Young adult, 16–24	581			
Older child, 14–15	109			
Child, 0-13	810			
Lone Parent premium	171			
Other PwC premium	383			
To finance the sum of gross transfers, 2020–21			£m	
ADD MARGIN in SCOTLAND for admin, HB, DBs etc.			£m	6,750
GRAND TOTAL for all SOCIAL SECURITY,			£m	

Note your objectives in designing your model.

What assumptions are you making?

Photocopy, or use pencil for, these tables.

Table B.1 UK Costing a BI model in £m for the UK, 2020–21

Col 1	Col 2	Col 3	Col 4 = Col 3 x365/7	Col 5 = Col 2 x Col 4 div by 1,000
Groups by age or premium	UK Population 2017 '000s	Your own BI Model, £ pw	Your own BI Model, £ pa	COST of your own BI Model £m
Whole population	66,436	—	—	—
Pensioner, 65 or over	12,166			
Working-age, 25–64	34,505			
Young adult, 16–24	7,141			
Older child, 14–15	1,445			
Child, 0-13	11,179			
Lone Parent premium	1,941			
Other PwC premium	4,913			
To finance the sum of gross transfers, 2020–21			£m	
ADD MARGIN in SCOTLAND for admin, HB, DBs etc.			£m	82,003
GRAND TOTAL for all SOCIAL SECURITY,			£m	

Table B.2 Scot A method for costing a BI model for Scotland in 2020–21 as an income tax rate

In 2018, mean gross income per head of man, woman and child, Y-BAR, in Scotland was £404.04 pw.

Col 1	Col 2	Col 3	Col 4	Col 3 x col 4
Groups by Age or premium	Scot Population 2018 '000s	Proportion of population	BI as proportion of av. income	Contribution to tax rate
65 +	1,026	0.18869		
25–64	2,911	0.53531		
16–24	582	0.10692		
14–15	109	0.02007		
0–13	810	0.14901		
All	5,438	1.00000	—	—
Lone P premium	171	0.03144		
Other PwC premium	383	0.07043		
To finance the sum of BIs, 2020–21,			t =	
ADD Scotland's MARGIN for admin, retained benefits etc. t =				+ 0.0587
GRAND TOTAL for all SOCIAL SECURITY,			t =	

Table B.2 UK A method for costing a BI model for the UK in 2020–21 as an income tax rate

In 2018, mean gross income per head of man woman and child, Y-BAR, in the UK was £471.69 pw.

Col 1	Col 2	Col 3	Col 4	Col 3 x col 4
Groups by Age or premium	UK Population 2018 '000s	Proportion of population	BI as proportion of av. income	Contribution to tax rate
65 or over	12,166	0.18312		
25–64	34,505	0.51937		
16–24	7,141	0.10749		
14–15	1,445	0.02175		
0–13	11,179	0.16827		
All	66,436	1.00000	—	—
Lone P premium	1,941	0.02922		
Other PwC premium	4,913	0.07395		
To finance the sum of BIs, 2020–21, t =				
ADD UK MARGIN for admin, retained benefits etc. t =				+ 0.0502
GRAND TOTAL for all SOCIAL SECURITY, t =				

Table B.3 BIs by household type (excluding Housing and Disability Benefits)

Column 1	Col 2	Col 3	Col 4	Col 5	Col 6
£ pw	An income floor:		AHC Poverty Benchmarks		Your own BI Model
Household Configuration		MTBs 2020–21	EU '17–18	MIS 2019	2020–21
Single pens	Pens Cred	173.75	152.08	177.87	
Couple pens		265.20	262.20	279.53	
Single W-age	JSA/ ESA	74.35	152.08	197.71	
Couple W-age		116.80	262.20	335.64	
Young adult, aged 16–24		58.90	152.08/ 110.12	197.71	
Lone Parent + toddler	JSA, CTC, CB	160.13	204.52	288.37	
LP + pre-sch + primary school		228.35	256.96	367.26	
LP + pre + prim + sec-sch		296.57	367.08	485.71	
Couple + toddler	JSA/ ESA, CTC, CB	202.58	314.64	374.67	
Couple + pre-sch + primary school		270.80	367.08	453.11	
Couple + pre-sch + prim + sec-sch		339.02	477.20	581.58	
Couple + all four		407.24	529.64	633.21	

APPENDIX C

'Excel' template for designing and costing your own BI model

The table below provides a template for creating the method, as described in chapter 10, for costing your own UK BI model, using Microsoft Excel. Save a copy of it, to which you can return each time you want to start a new model.

For Scotland, use the 'Save As' instruction to save a copy of this file. In cells D16–D22, substitute the population figures for Scotland, as given in Table 10.2 Scot, including the figures for boys and girls aged 14–15, and for 'parents with care'. Insert the figure for income, £m, in Scotland from Table A.2 into F6, the margin for Scotland from Table B.2 Scot into F26 and update B4. D24 is the UK figure divided by 12.

Each year, the population figures, D16–D22, and D24 (the population aged 16 or over who have an annual gross income greater than 0, calculated in chapter 11) need to be updated. The 'SUM' in E16 provides a method for checking that the population figures are correct. It should add up to 1.0. Also update the income figure in F6, and the margin in F26, together with B5, B6, F5 and D14. The benchmark figures in columns D32–D45, E32–E45 and F32–F45 should also be updated (see chapter 8).

The input cells are B17–B22, into which you can insert proportions between 0 and 1 inclusive, or your weekly money values divided by C6 (Y-BAR). A value for a Personal Allowance can be inserted into C24.

The key output cells are F17–F22 (which give the contributions of each age group to the tax rate), and F23–F27 which give the rates of restructured income tax necessary to finance the BI model. Cells C35–C45 record the resulting BI allocations for different household types. These can be compared with your chosen benchmark in column D, E or F. You can use the 'border' facility to outline the sets of input and output cells.

Table C Excel template for designing and costing your own preferred BI model for the UK.

	A	B	C
1			
2	CALCULATE	the STANDARD INCOME	TAX rate
3			
4	AREA	UK	
5	FISCAL YEAR	2020–21	
6	Y-BAR for year	2018.	=D6*7/365
7			£ pw
8			
9			
10	TABLE	TO CALCULATE THE	COST IN
11	Insert a value	between 0 and 1 inclusive	into cells
12			
13		INPUT	
14	Sub groups	BI / Y-BAR	BI £ pw
15			
16	POPULATION		
17	Aged 65 or over	=189/C6	=B17*C6
18	Aged 25–64	=151.2/C6	=B18*C6
19	Aged 16–24	=151.2/C6	=B19*C6
20	Aged 14–15	=75.6/C6	=B20*C6
21	Aged 0–13	=75.6/C6	=B21*C6
22	PwCs	=37.8/C6	=B22*C6
23	Gross Transfers		
24	PERS ALLOW of		3120
25	Total so far		

	D	E	F
1			
2	NEEDED to	FINANCE your	BI MODEL
3			
4			INCOME
5			IN 2018
6	=F6*1000000/D16		1634013
7	£ pa		in £ millions
8			
9			
10	TERMS OF THE	INCOME TAX	RATE
11	B17 to B22, or	=weekly money	value/C6
12			
13	POPULATION	POPULATION	COST IN
14	IN 2018	PROPORTION	income tax rate
15			OUTPUT
16	66435550	=SUM(E17:E21)	
17	12165557	=D17/D16	=B17*E17
18	34504722	=D18/D16	=B18*E18
19	7141092	=D19/D16	=B19*E19
20	1445217	=D20/D16	=B20*E20
21	11178962	=D21/D16	=B21*E21
22	6854335	=D22/D16	=B22*E22
23			=SUM(F17:F22)
24	45382371	=C24*D24/1000000	=E24*F23/F6
25			=F23+F24

26	Add MARGIN		
27	GRAND TOTAL		
28			
29	TABLE	COMPARING YOUR BI	MODEL
30			
31		YOUR OUTPUT	OUTPUT
32		as a proportion	for your
33	HOUSEHOLD	of Y-BAR	BI MODEL
34	TYPES		£ pw
35	Single pens	=B17	=B35*C6
36	Couple pens	=B17*2	=B36*C6
37	Single w-age	=B18	=B37*C6
38	Couple w-age	=B18*2	=B38*C6
39	Lone Parent + 1	=B18+B22+B21	=B39*C6
40	Lone Parent + 2	=B18+B22+B21*2	=B40*C6
41	Lone Parent + 3	=B18+B22+B21*2+B20	=B41*C6
42	Couple + 1	=B18*2+B22+B21	=B42*C6
43	Couple + 2	=B18*2+B22+B21*2	=B43*C6
44	Couple + 3	=B18*2+B22+B21*2+B20	=B44*C6
45	Couple + 4	=B18*2+B22+B21*3+B20	=B45*C6

26			0.0502
27			=F25+F26
28			
29	WITH	VARIOUS	BENCHMARKS
30			
31			
32	MTBs 2020–21	EU 2017–18	MIS 2019
33	excl. HB and CTS	AHC	AHC
34	£ pw	£ pw	£ pw
35	173.75	152.08	177.87
36	265.20	262.2	279.53
37	74.35	152.08	197.71
38	116.80	262.2	335.64
39	160.13	204.52	288.37
40	228.35	256.96	367.26
41	296.57	367.08	485.71
42	202.58	314.64	374.67
43	270.80	367.08	453.11
44	339.02	477.2	581.58
45	407.24	529.64	633.21

Refer to chapter 8 to see how the official EU poverty benchmark is calculated.

APPENDIX D

Chronology of basic income with respect to the UK

The references for this chronology are given in full in *A Basic Income Handbook*.

The website of the Citizen's Basic Income Trust (CBIT) gives access to an excellent archive of material charting the development of BI in the UK over the last 30 years (www.citizensincome.org).

Basic Income Earth Network (BIEN) has a very comprehensive review of the history of BI on its website (www.basicincome.org/basic-income/history).

Aristotle (384–22 BC) thought that men are fundamentally unequal and therefore the distribution of income and wealth should reflect that. His views were based on expediency, on what works for a State as a whole, rather than moral principle. But democracy works better without extremes of poverty and wealth, and in particular poverty is the parent of revolution and crime (White, 2000).

The foundation of all the great faiths in the world is that of compassion, expressed as loving kindness (*Metta*, Buddhism), and caring for the poor is a religious duty for all the Abrahamic faiths. Jesus' second greatest commandment is 'Love thy neighbour as thyself' and is found in three of the Gospels (Mark 12:29-31, Matthew 19:19, Luke 10:27). 'It is more blessed to give than to receive' (Acts 20:35). The miracle of the feeding of the 5,000 could be interpreted as Jesus persuading the crowd to share what they had with their neighbours (Mark 6:30-44). Similarly, Jesus' parable of the labourers in the vineyard, where all received the same day's wage whether they worked for a full or part day, acknowledges the fact that all of the workers needed the full day's wage to provide for their families (Matthew 20:1-16).

1516: Thomas More (1478–1535) was the author of *Utopia*, published in Latin in two volumes in Louvain, Belgium. He regarded the punishment of death for the crime of stealing food as disproportionate, and suggested that some means of livelihood, guaranteed by the government to all the members of a particular community, was a better cure for theft (BIEN).

1601: The Poor Law of England and Wales was enacted in 1601. It was a system that included out-relief, condemnation to the dreaded Poor House, and the hiring out of paupers at cheap rates to employers – all designed to act as a deterrent from claiming off the parish. However, this latter practice was believed to depress wages to the detriment of independent workers. In 1795, a code of out-relief was introduced in Speenhamland, a village in Berkshire, which topped up the wages of workers to the poverty level. This, too, was believed to lead employers to pay unduly low wages, forcing workers to claim relief.

1652: The Religious Society of Friends (Quakers), has had a Testimony to Equality since its early days in the mid-17th century. 'We are not for names, nor men, nor titles of Government, nor are we for this party nor against the other... but we are for justice and mercy and truth and peace and true freedom, that these may be exalted in our nation, and that goodness, righteousness, meekness, temperance, peace and unity with God, and with one another, that these things may abound. Edward Burrough, 1659' (*Quaker Faith and Practice*, 1995: para 23.11). Quakers put out a public statement in 1987 that is still relevant today: 'We are angered by actions which have knowingly led to the polarisation of our country – into the affluent, who epitomise success according to the values of a materialistic society, and the "have-leasts", who by the expectations of that same society are oppressed, judged, found wanting and punished' (*Quaker Faith and Practice*, 1995: para 23.21).

1796: Thomas Paine (1737–1809) wrote in his pamphlet *Agrarian Justice*,

> The earth, in its natural uncultivated state was, and ever would have continued to be, *the common property of the human race.*

The introduction of private property added, through cultivation, a 'tenfold' value to created earth. At the same time, however, it dispossessed more than half the inhabitants of every nation of their natural inheritance, without providing... an indemnification for that loss, and has thereby created a species of poverty and wretchedness that did not exist before.

Every proprietor 'of cultivated land' owed to the community a ground rent for the land that he held. With this sum, Paine aimed to set up a National Fund, out of which there would be paid to every person,

> when arrived at the age of 21 years, the sum of £15, as a compensation in part, for the loss of his or her natural inheritance, by the system of landed property' and 'the sum of ten pounds per annum, during life, to every person now living, of age 50 years, and to all others as they shall arrive at that age.

This system... would so organise civilisation 'that the whole weight of misery can be removed'. It would aid the blind, the lame and the aged poor, and at the same time guarantee that the new generation would never become poor. And all this would not be achieved through charity. 'It is not charity, but a right... not bounty but justice, that I am pleading for'. (Paine (1796) 1974: 37).

1849: John Stuart Mill (1806–73) regarded inequality of income and wealth as a great evil, but he did not agree with giving the role of redistribution to the state. He wanted to protect wealth earned by the free use of mind or body, through effort or saving, but he was prepared to limit large inheritances, and he favoured taxing land. He thought that free education for the poor was a good method of obtaining greater equality. He was a utilitarian who thought that there were different levels of utility, and that the same unit of income gave greater utility to a poor person than to a rich one, thus inciting what later became known as the 'law of diminishing marginal utility of income' (White, 2000).

1879: Henry George (1839–97) wrote *Progress and Poverty: An Inquiry into the Cause of Industrial Depressions and the Increase of Want with the Increase in Wealth – The Remedy*. He claimed that 'as an economy grows, labourers do not share in the economic growth, but instead are reduced to poverty, because of increased rents to landowners' (White, 2000: 22). The remedy that he advocated is a Land Value Tax.

1918: Bertrand Russell (1872–1970) wrote *Roads to Freedom, Socialism, Anarchism and Syndicalism*, in which he expressed a wish to combine the advantages of socialism and anarchism. He proposed that 'a certain small income, sufficient for necessaries, should be secured to all, whether they work or not, and that a larger income – as much larger as might be warranted by the total amount of commodities produced – should be given to those who are willing to engage in some work which the community recognises as useful… When education is finished, no one should be compelled to work and those who choose not to work should receive a bare livelihood and be left completely free' (BIEN, 'Russell's combination of anarchism and socialism').

1918: Dennis Milner (1892–1956), a young Quaker in his mid-twenties, presented his *Scheme for a State Bonus for All* to the *War and Social Order Committee* of the *Yearly Meeting* of the Religious Society of Friends in May 1918, and wrote a pamphlet with his wife, Mabel (Milner et al, 1918). The **State Bonus** was pitched at 20 per cent of GDP *per cap*. Despite further writings (Pickard, 1919) (Milner, 1920), and a supporting State Bonus League, the campaign was short-lived, ending after being rejected by the Labour Party Annual Conference in June 1921. This 'is in all probability the earliest full-blown modern basic incomes proposal' (Van Trier, 1995: 31). Van Trier examines Milner's scheme in detail, noting how it contains all the qualities of, and arguments for, BI schemes that were developed independently later in the twentieth century.

1921: 'Major' Clifford Hugh Douglas (1879–1952) was a British engineer, and amateur economist who introduced the idea of a **National Dividend** (Van Trier, 1995: 190). However, 'the first time Major Douglas released a real blue-print of a policy proposal was as late as 11 March 1932, when he published a set of proposals in the *Glasgow Evening Times*, titled '"A Draft Social Credit Scheme for Scotland"' (Van Trier, 199: 191–2). It was to be financed 'not from borrowing from banks, neither from taxation. It will be '"created for the State by the banks and paid out by the State's direction"' (Van Trier, 1995: 308). Douglas described his Social Credit movement as an interdisciplinary, distributive philosophy. It did not find favour in the UK, but the Social Credit Party governed Alberta, Canada, from 1935–71, although it soon dropped its National Dividend proposal (BIEN, Major Douglas and the Social Credit Movement).

1936: Both James Meade (1907–95), winner of the Nobel Prize in economics in 1977, and GDH Cole (1889–1959) used the term '**social dividend**' in 1935. Meade used it throughout his life, but implied different things at different times (Van Trier, 1995: 363). 'And it was to become a crucial component of the Agathatopia Project to which he devoted his last writings

(1989, 1993, 1995)' (BIEN, 'Cole and Meade on Social Dividend').
'Social Dividend' was the term commonly used until the early
1980s, when the term 'Basic Income' became popular.

1942: William Beveridge was a Liberal peer, and a Director
of LSE, who designed a new system of social protection for
the nation, largely replacing the existing piecemeal
provision. His *Report on Social Insurance and Allied
Services* (1942) was a best seller, and his proposals were
passed into law in the National Insurance Act 1946 and
National Assistance Act 1948. It spread more slowly to other
European nations. This dual system has embodied the
Social Security system in the UK from that date.

1943: Juliet Rhys Williams, also a Liberal peer, developed
her Social Contract at the same time as Beveridge was
writing his report. It was designed to solve the problems of
the distribution of wealth, the freeing of the unemployed to
undertake part-time work for profit, to preserve national
unity and the complete abolition of the Means Test, among
others (Rhys Williams, 1943: 138). It is based on the principle
that '*The prevention of want must be regarded as being the
duty of the State to all its citizens, and not merely a favoured
few*'. It comprised a work-tested 'benefit... of 21 shillings per
week to a man, 19 shillings per week to his wife, or to a
single woman, *paid in her own right and not merely as a
dependent*, and 10 shillings in respect of each of his children
under 18' (Rhys Williams, 1943: 145, italics in original). Her
son, Brandon, a Conservative MP, wrote *The New Social
Contract* (Rhys Williams, 1967).

1945: The Universal Declaration of Human Rights was
adopted by the General Assembly of the United Nations in
Paris on 10 December 1945. Article 25 (1) states

> everyone has the right to a standard of living adequate
> for the health and well-being of himself and of his

family, including food, clothing, housing and medical care and necessary social services, and the right to security in the event of unemployment, sickness, disability, old age or other lack of livelihood in circumstances beyond his control'.

This was incorporated into the European Convention on Human Rights set up in Rome in 1950 (United Nations, 1945).

There were few other writings about a Social Dividend in the UK before the mid-1980s, except for (Brown et al, 1969) (Atkinson, 1969: chapter 9) (Meade, 1972) (Atkinson, 1973) and (Roberts, 1981).

1968–80: There were four income maintenance experiments in the USA in the late 1960s and 1970s.

1972: The Heath Government's *Proposals for a Tax-Credit System*, Cmnd 5116, was an unexpected development, but it was not based on the individual. Its aims were a) 'to simplify and reform the whole system of personal tax collection', and b) 'to improve the system of income support for poor people' (Green Paper, 1972: para 7). The proposal was examined in detail by Atkinson, and rejected because 'there are important low-income groups who would be given little help or actually lose from the Green Paper proposals' (Atkinson, 1973: 61).

1974: The Liberal Party Manifesto, published in February 1974, expressed six aims, of which the first was:

> Establish the universal right to a *minimum income* balanced by a fairer *distribution of wealth*, through a credit income tax system and national minimum earnings guarantees (page 1).

> It would '... replace most of the 44 means tests to which under-privileged and handicapped people are subjected... All income would be taxed according to a

progressive scale from the very first pound, but *everyone* would be entitled to various 'credits' or allowances depending on circumstances.' (Italics in the original) (Liberal Party, 1974:10).

In March 1983, the Liberal Party published its Tax Credit Plan (Vince, 1983). Parker compared the schemes of the Liberal and the Social Democratic Parties for 1982-83 (Parker, 1984) (Parker, 1989).

1974-9: The Mincome Program experiment was carried out in Dauphin, Manitoba, Canada.

1976: The Alaska Permanent Fund was set up based on oil royalties and other oil revenues, that were invested in international markets.

1982: Alaska Permanent Fund Dividend was first distributed.

1982-3: The House of Commons Treasury and Civil Service Committee conducted their 'Enquiry into the Structure of Personal Income Taxation and Income Support'. A sub-committee chaired by Michael Meacher MP received Memorandums from several sources, which were published in a third special report (House of Commons, 1983). The Committee recommended further study of integrated tax/benefit systems.

1984: The Basic Income Research Group (BIRG) was formed. It became a charity in 1989, and changed its name to Citizen's Income Trust (CIT) in 1993, and again to Citizen's Basic Income Trust (CBIT) in 2017. Its objectives were, and still are, to 'advance public education about the national economic and social effects and influences of Basic Income Systems'. It maintains a website with an excellent archive and a library, and has published a regular Bulletin or Newsletter for the last three and a half decades.

1986: The Basic Income European Network (BIEN) was founded in Louvain-la-Neuve in 1986. BIEN is a loose network of national organisations, which maintains a very informative website, www.basicincome.org, and has organised a Congress every two years. Its General Assembly in Seoul in July 2016 agreed to hold congresses annually. Publication of the proceedings of each congress has contributed greatly to the literature available in the subject. In 2004, the General Assembly of BIEN agreed to a proposal to change its name to Basic Income *Earth* Network, to reflect its extension of affiliated organisation status to countries outside Europe. With the support of other BI organisations, it set up the e-journal *Basic Income Studies* in 2006.

1986-present: Some key contributions about BI have been made by Van Der Veen and Van Parijs (1986), Rhys Williams (1989), Parker (1989), Walter (1989), Brittan and Webb (1990), Atkinson (1995), Van Parijs (1995), Van Trier (1995), Fitzpatrick (1999), McKay (2005), Standing (2011), Torry (2013), Torry (2015), Van Parijs and Vanderborght (2017), Standing (2017), Miller (2017), Downes and Lansley (eds) (2018), Torry (2018) and Haagh (2019).

2004: Brazil sanctioned the conditional *Bolsa Familia* into law.

2005: The World Bank published its report about the wealth of a nation.

2008-9: Privately-financed BI pilot experiment in Otjivero, Namibia.

2010-6: Iran introduces *de facto* a BI scheme based on oil wealth.

2011-3: BI pilot experiments in India.

2012-4: The European Union introduced a new instrument, the European Citizens' Initiative (ECI) in 2012. An ECI on

Unconditional Basic Income (ECI on UBI) was registered on 14 January 2013. Although it only obtained 285,000 signatures across the 28 countries of the EU within the ensuing year, it raised the profile of the idea with the public across the EU. The work of promoting the concept of a BI in Europe continues via UBI-Europe. (www.basicincome-europe.org/ubie).

2013: Basic Income UK (BI-UK), which was set up while campaigning in the UK for the ECI on UBI, is the focus for a network of grassroots groups in the UK, who are interested in the idea of, and wish to campaign for, a BI (www.basicincome.org.uk).

2014: This year saw a significant increase in public events relating to BI. In January, the Scottish Parliament hosted a seminar and round-table on BI for MSPs and other interested parties. In March, the House of Commons hosted a similar event, and CIT organised a successful BI conference at the British Library, London, in June. The Scottish Green Party published details of a BI scheme for Scotland in August 2014. BI is also part of a long-term policy for the Green Party in England and Wales.

2015-8: There has been an increase in interest in BI in recent years, probably in response to the changing labour market conditions, the concern about increasing automation and robotisation, increasing inequality in income and wealth in many countries around the world, and the growing incidence of poverty. This is evidenced by the large number of books in which a BI is referred to as, at least, a partial solution to the problem being explored (Wilkinson *et al*, 2009: 264) (Dorling, 2011: 267) (Skidelsky *et al*, 2012: 197-202) (Mason, 2015: 284-6) (Murphy, 2015: 192-5) (Srnicek *et al*, 2015: chapter 6) (Sayer, 2016: 361) and (Bregman, 2017). In addition, several reports exploring the desirability and feasibility of BI, with some proposing their own schemes for the UK, have been produced recently by some think tanks and others (Painter et al, 2015) (Mackenzie et al, 2016) (Reed et al, 2016], [Miller, 2017], [Torry, 2017, 2018b], [Painter et al, 2019], [Standing, 2019] and [Lansley et al, 2019].

2015: The National Welfare Charter was launched at the TUC Congress, calling for an increase in 'the numbers of people who support the principle of a minimum Citizen's Income for all'. A new organisation, the Citizen's Basic Income Network Scotland (CBINS), with the educational objective of disseminating information to the public and policy-makers alike, about the desirability and feasibility of a BI in a more fiscally-devolved or independent Scotland, was set up and granted charitable status in February 2016.

2016: Delegates at the Scottish National Party (SNP) spring conference in March agreed to a motion proposed by Ronnie Cowan MP supporting the introduction of a basic income in Scotland. In June, the Shadow Chancellor, John McDonnell, said that the Labour Party is considering backing a universal basic income as part of its new economic policy. Ronnie Cowan MP (SNP) won the right to hold the first debate about BI in the Westminster Parliament, which took place on 14 September in Westminster Hall. A stronger TUC motion called for support for a Universal BI.

2016: Switzerland's Referendum on 5 June rejected its Basic Income proposal.

2017: Finland's two-year targeted income experiment began in January. The Scottish Social Security Committee heard oral evidence regarding BI on 9 March at Holyrood. On 22 May, the Green Party of England and Wales included a BI scheme in its manifesto for the General Election on 8 June. Four Scottish Councils agreed to explore the feasibility of conducting a BI pilot experiment together. On 5 September, the Scottish Government committed £250,000 as seed-corn finance for the planning stage of the experiment, from April 2018 to April 2020.

2018: The Scottish Government approved the *Application for Funding* submitted by the Scottish CBI Feasibility Study Steering Group. A Cross Party Group on Basic Income was granted official status by the Scottish Parliament on 7 June. In August, the new provincial government in Ontario, Canada, announced the cancellation of its experiment by the end of March 2019, despite its assurances to the contrary before its election. The Secretary General of the UN endorsed basic income on 25 September.

2019: Initial analysis of the results from the first year of the Finnish experiment indicate that the BIs have not made any significant difference to the recipients' labour market participation, but they feel much happier. The report commissioned by the Shadow Chancellor of the Exchequer on the feasibility of BI pilot experiments in the UK was presented in May (Standing, 2019). In October, the Citizen's Basic Income Feasibility Study Steering Group published its very thorough interim report of world-leading research in preparation for potential BI pilot projects in Scotland.

2020: There were numerous calls for Basic Income schemes to be implemented around the world, following the onset of the coronavirus Covid-19 pandemic. Webinars in Finnish and English presenting the final results of the Finnish experiment became available on 6 May via https://www.kela.fi/web/en/final-results-of-the-finnish-basic-income-experiment/.

APPENDIX E

'Aye, but...'

SOME REGARD THE IDEA of Basic Income as utopian folly, and it will be difficult to persuade them of its viability. Others would like to be persuaded, but have nagging doubts. It goes without saying that criticism of a particular model does not necessarily constitute an objection to the generic BI. Here, I present counter arguments to some of the objections to, criticisms of, and scepticism about, basic income, commonly expressed as 'Aye, but...'

The current National Insurance (NI) system is good enough and just needs tweaking at the edges.

The coverage of the NI system is very incomplete:

- The NI earnings-replacement benefits are paid only to earners;
- If there is a gap in the contribution record, then the NI benefits are reduced;
- Some people are unable to contribute at all, due to their unpaid care-giving roles;
- Self-employed people receive very limited protection from the NI system.

You can alleviate poverty by increasing benefit levels, without having to change the whole system.

This is not true. The increase in the NI benefits will not reach those who are excluded from the NI system, or who are covered inadequately. Also the structural flaws in the means-tested SA safety net prevent poverty alleviation. For instance, the assessment and delivery of benefits being based on the couple prevents many women from accessing benefits in their own right.

If you have the individual as the unit of assessment and delivery, couples would receive more than they need.

Individual assessment is absolutely crucial to emancipate married and other cohabiting women from the trap of financial dependence. Individual assessment is accepted currently for other adults sharing accommodation, so why not for couples? Acceptance that couples will receive more than they need, known as household economies of scale (HES) and an integral part of many BI schemes, could acknowledge that living with other people can be stressful and that compromises are needed. The availability of HES could provide an incentive for adults to share accommodation and reduce demand for single person housing.

Surely a BI is just a feminist system?

A BI income system treats men and women equally. The current NI and SA systems are so misogynistic that, by contrast, a BI could appear to precipitate a feminist revolution.

A BI system will force women back into their kitchens.

Some women fear that a BI system would encourage other women, particularly those in soul-destroying, low-paid, insecure, drudge jobs, to leave the paid work-force in favour of spending more time at home, caring for children and elders, a privilege enjoyed by some wealthier women. The same choice would face both men and women. A BI system together with better education and skills-training for women are the preferred solutions here.

Why give a BI to rich people who don't need it?

Those who dislike the idea of giving a BI to rich people must be absolutely apoplectic about their receiving tax breaks in proportion to their incomes. Presumably their anxiety levels would subside if these perks were withdrawn, in favour of giving everyone the same level of BI.

Using a BI to help to create a more inclusive society must include giving a BI to rich people, but they would not necessarily be better off, if they were taxed more progressively than at present. It is more efficient to assess people once only each year for income tax, rather than for a second time for benefits. Targeting does not protect poor people but segregates them and can make them more vulnerable. A universal system from which both rich and poor can benefit, like the NHS, is more likely to be promoted by rich people, and at the same time will protect poorer people.

Should asylum seekers receive a BI?

Currently, asylum seekers in the UK receive little help from the state, but some may receive support from charities, while others are left destitute. A case could be made for treating them more humanely on compassionate grounds, by granting them a BI on registration and speeding up the process of assessing their claims for refugee status. The BI would only be withdrawn a few weeks after his/her application or appeal has been rejected, when she/he is required to depart.

Will a BI encourage illegal immigration?

A BI could be paid to anyone who fulfils the eligibility criteria, such as:

- They have the legal right to permanent residence in the country;
- They have fulfilled a minimum period of continuous legal and physical residence in the country prior to commencement of payment; and
- They maintain a continuing physical presence in the country for most of each subsequent year, while in receipt of the BI.

This would be quite a tough call for most illegal immigrants. An international BI system could give people in poorer countries the opportunity to develop their own economies, reducing the incentive to emigrate.

People's lives and needs are too complex to be met by a single simple system.

This is true. Universal Credit provides extra support to cover dependents including children, childcare costs, housing costs and disability payments. With a BI system, partners will receive their own BIs, and children will receive a child BI. Separate but parallel systems would have to be retained to meet housing costs, and the costs often incurred by disabled people.

One of the aims of a BI system is to end means-testing, but you can't do this while retaining means-tested housing benefits. So, is it worth implementing a BI?

Getting rid of means-testing is not the only aim of a BI system. A BI system could reduce entitlement to, and thus expenditure on, MTBs, depending on its generosity. The need to retain an individualised Housing Benefit as a separate but parallel means-tested system is the result of the housing policy that has been pursued in the UK for the last four decades and is not a problem caused by the Social Security system. When a more appropriate housing policy has been adopted, and the system rectified, then an element to cover housing costs could be considered for inclusion in the BI.

Why give 'something for nothing'? What about reciprocity?

Most of the value of our economy is built on the contributions of all our forebears. Rather than being 'something for nothing', a BI reclaims the rights of the people to their share of the natural resources of the land.

The amount of the BI will never provide for more than people's basic needs and everyone should be entitled to his/her necessities, otherwise their lives are shortened. Unconditional BI values all citizens and treats them with respect. A BI system would bring out the best in people, inducing a reciprocal desire to contribute to society through, for example, care or community work.

A BI system will discourage people from working-for-pay. What about free-riders?

Both unearned incomes (including a BI) and marginal deductions from earnings act as incentive effects on a person's willingness to work-for-pay, and they interact in complex ways. There will still be plenty of incentives for people to work-for-pay. A BI will cover only basic needs at most. Luxuries will still have to be earned. Most people want to work, not only for the earnings, but also for the many social and health advantages that it provides. Rather than foisting unwilling workers on otherwise efficient companies, a small number of free-riders could be tolerated as long as they do no harm, and their critics could choose to do likewise.

Since the BIs are not means-tested, they will restore the incentive to work-for-pay contained in the net wage rate, which should have positive incentive effects on low-wage workers. Some higher-waged workers may choose to work less in order to achieve a better work-life balance. There could be a redistribution of an individual's hours between paid and unpaid work. Wage rates are likely to adjust.

Will wage protection still be required?

Economic theory claims that there is a price which will equate supply and demand. However, in the labour market, it could occur at wage rates that are so low that workers could not maintain themselves, or earn their way out of poverty. Situations such as these justify wage protection, like the National Living Wage, to ensure that workers can earn enough to live on, to supplement a partial BI.

Will automation lead to mass unemployment?

Although much debated, no one knows the answer to this question. Only time will tell. Certainly, automation has already changed the labour market significantly in the last few years or decades. The days when most men could look forward to a life time of well-paid full employment, as in the post WWII era, are unlikely to return. It will be prudent to be prepared to face possible changes, by:

- making sure that everyone has enough to live on;
- taxing the returns to capital that could increase if automation continues; and
- continuing to reduce income and wealth inequalities that are otherwise likely to increase.

John Kay (2017: 72) claims that 'either the level of basic income is unacceptably low, or the cost of providing [an earnings-replacement level] is unacceptably high'.

Kay points out that the cost of a BI, that would be sufficient for a household, is unacceptably high – but BI is a benefit designed for an *individual*! Claiming that 'the level of basic income is unacceptably low' ignores the fact that there are millions of people on below-poverty incomes, for whom even that lower level of BI (that would help to prevent or at least reduce poverty) would be very acceptable!

We can't afford a basic income system. It will cost too much.

How much is too much? Can we afford not to? How rich does the UK have to be before it is prepared to support the most vulnerable in society effectively? What is the price of a good society? The cost will depend on the generosity of the scheme. An introductory BI scheme embedded in the current UK Social Security system could easily be afforded. In chapter 10, it is demonstrated that a moderate scheme could have been financed in 2020–21 by a restructured income tax system with a flat rate of income tax of 37 per cent for the UK, or of 38 per cent for a fiscally-devolved Scotland.

More importantly, a generous scheme based on a full BI of 0.4 of mean gross income for all adults and a child BI of 0.2 for all dependent children aged 0–15, with a small personal allowance, could be implemented for as little as a flat rate of income tax of 45 or 46 per cent. This is a lower rate of income tax plus NI contributions than some people pay at the moment, and the majority of the population would gain financially. This system could be possible if future governments refrained from favouring wealthier people in proportion to their incomes via income tax breaks, and instead distributed the Social Security and tax welfare budgets more equally as a BI. This could be achievable, if the scheme were to be implemented gradually over a fixed period of time. Ultimately, it will depend on what tax rate citizens are prepared to pay for a better society.

Will rich people (threaten to) emigrate if income tax rates rise?

Rich people enjoy living in the UK with its political stability, temperate climate, English language, and cultural diversity. It is not obvious where they would go. How many left when an additional rate of income tax of 0.50 was introduced in the fiscal year 2010–11? Employees of international companies enjoy working in the Nordic countries, in spite of high income tax rates.

Will a BI system be inflationary?

If the BI system were financed by printing money, and if the regular input of money supply into the economy were not balanced by a similar regular withdrawal through taxation, then it would be inflationary. As long as the BI system is funded by taxation which withdraws income from the richer section of the population and transfers it to a poorer part, then it is not expected to be inflationary. However, if there were shortages, then wage rates and thence prices of some goods could rise. Since the housing stock changes only slowly, there could be a risk of some rent increases initially.

BI ideas seem to attract people from both the right and left of the political spectrum. How can it do both?

A BI income is not about just a single objective. It can help to achieve emancipation, poverty-prevention and redistribution of income. Not means-testing benefits can help the labour market to work more efficiently, and it can simplify the administration of a social security system, making it less intrusive. This combination of equity, community, efficiency and choice goals can appeal to both left and right of the political spectrum, but with different priorities.

Some free-market billionaires promote the idea of a BI, using it as an excuse to undermine the rest of the welfare state, by underfunding or privatising public welfare services. Is it worth the risk?

A BI system and universal basic services are not alternatives, but complement each other. The welfare state in the UK has been slowly (or not so slowly) and surely underfunded and privatised before our very eyes by recent Westminster governments. Rejecting a BI will not stop this process. The only way is to reclaim our democracy, and to fight for both the BI and to turn the tide on the dismantling of our public welfare services, on which most of us depend.

Some people quite like the idea of a BI system, but are sceptical that it will ever get off the ground, or, even if it does, that it will ever attain a significant level.

It stands as a warning to all that the amounts of the NI and social assistance benefits, after the accolades that greeted their introduction, have been consistently eroded over time. It is clear that a BI will need some constitutional safeguards, to protect the system from being sabotaged, or completely overturned, leaving the public unprotected, and also to protect BIs from erosion. Similarly, protection is required to make it illegal for individuals to use their BIs as security for any loan that could risk their being thrown into poverty by the loss of a lifetime income stream. Also, BIs should be protected from debt collection.

Many people fear change. A BI system could undermine hard-won workers' rights and solidarity.

The unknown can induce fear. Things may not turn out as claimed. There are likely to be some unanticipated consequences. Some people may lose more than others. But it is the automation revolution, if it continues, rather than a BI system, that is more likely to threaten hard-won workers' rights and solidarity. Change is happening now, and will continue to occur. The most prudent strategy is to prepare for it as well as possible, and minimise our maximum regrets. The UK Social Security system is broken and is not fit for purpose. If the public is as well-informed as possible, and people are familiar with the desirability and feasibility of a BI system, and are also aware of any real objections, then they will be better able to decide for themselves whether the advantages outweigh any disadvantages.

If a BI is such a good idea, why has no developed nation implemented it already?

The post WWII introduction of the National Insurance and Social Assistance systems by many European and other countries was such a success, compared with what went before, that it has taken a long time to convince politicians that it is no longer working well, despite mounting evidence. The disastrous implementation of Universal Credit in the UK has made the government wary of introducing such a radical approach to Social Security as a BI without evidence of its likely effects, and before there is popular demand for it from an informed public.

MAIN SOURCES OF DATA FOR THE UK AND SCOTLAND

Brief details are given here. Finding and accessing data can be one of the most time-consuming and frustrating parts of the exercise of examining facts and figures for Social Security in general, and BIs in particular. For further details about accessing the sources, the reader is referred to the 'Sources of Data' section at the end of *A Basic Income Handbook*.

Government sources

Many of the data files published by government sources can be downloaded using Microsoft Excel software, by googling the name of the data file, table or reference code.

Population

Mid-year UK and Scotland population estimates

- The database 'Population Estimates for UK, England and Wales, Scotland and Northern Ireland' is published annually by the ONS. Access Table MYE2: Population estimates by single year of age and sex for local authorities in the UK, mid-xxxx, where xxxx is the year. The Scottish data start at around row 399 or 400.

Census data 2011 for numbers of lone parents, and other responsible parents of dependent children aged 0–15

- Population figures by age giving this information can be obtained from Census 2011 data for the different UK nations, by googling the reference code, eg 'DC1118EW' or 'DC1118SC'.

United Kingdom National Accounts, The Blue Book, ONS, 2017–9 editions.

Google the name of the dataset required. The latest figures from each of the 2017–9 editions were extracted, which were the figures that were available at the time when decisions would have been needed. It is usually available in July or August each year. For the 2017 edition, each chapter must be downloaded separately:

- 'Chapter 1: National Accounts at a glance';
- 'Chapter 5: General Government';
- 'Chapter 6: Households and Non-Profit Institutions Serving Households', and
- 'Chapter 10: Public Sector Supplementary Tables'.

Each variable has its own unique four-letter reference code beside it. This is essential for abstracting the figures for all of the following series from the 2017–19 editions of the *Blue Book*. Click on the 'edit' button, and then use the 'find' facility and the four-letter reference code to locate the relevant series. Data for the following variables were accessed:

- **UK GDP** = Gross Domestic Product (production method) at market prices, series YBHA (originally from Table 1.2).

- **UK GDP per capita** = GDP per head of man, woman and child, series IHXT (originally from Table 1.5).

- Use the reference codes given in Appendix A above for the numbers who are **economically active** (self-employed, employees, unemployed) and the totals who were economically active and economically inactive (originally from Table 1.5).

- **UK Income** = 'Total Resources of Households and Non-Profit Institutions Serving Households', series QWMF (originally from Table 6.1.3). Used for creating Y-BAR for the UK.

- **Social Security Transfer Payments for the UK** were originally obtained from *Blue Book* Tables 5.1.4, 5.2.4S and 5.3.4S. Refer to Table 10.1, or Appendix A above for the reference codes.
- **UK Taxes and their Yields** were originally obtained from *Blue Book* Table 10.1. Refer to Table 10.1 above and Appendix A for the reference codes. You will need the following codes to create 'Other current taxes': NSFA, NRQB, E8A6, IY90, KIH3 and NMHK.

Scottish National Accounts Project (SNAP)

This offers a new experimental data set, *Quarterly National Accounts Scotland*. Google 'SNAP/QNAS'.

- **Scottish GDP at market prices**, and **GDP per capita** for each year were abstracted from Table A: Summary Gross Domestic Product Measures. The more conservative 'on shore' version was used, as opposed to the versions based on population or geographical shares of *extra-regio* (offshore) activity.
- **Scottish Income** was abstracted from Table I: Households and Non-Profit Institutions Serving Household (NPISHs) Sectors, Income Accounts: The Balance of Gross Primary Income = Compensation of Employees + Gross Operating Surplus and Mixed Income + Gross Property Income − Total Primary Uses.
  Used for creating Y-BAR for Scotland.

Department for Work and Pensions (DWP):

Households Below Average Income is published annually around March each year. Google 'HBAI 20xx/20yy' where xx and yy are consecutive years.

Select:

a) *Households Below Average Income: an analysis of the income distribution 1994/95 to 20xx/yy.pdf*: and the

b) *Supporting data tables*, comprising Excel data files.

Mean and median equivalised household incomes (BHC and AHC)

- The 2015/16, 2016/17 and 2017/18 figures for the median (BHC and AHC) and mean (BHC) are available on page 3 of the report, but the mean (AHC) figures had to be accessed via Excel Table 2.1 AHC.

Proposed Benefit and Pension Rates.

- **Means-tested benefit rates** – various

'Benefit Expenditure and Caseload Tables 2019'.

Download the 'Outturn and forecast: Autumn Statement 2019 (XLS)' file, to obtain the current expenditures in 2018 on benefits that would be retained (which would be components of the margin that is added to the cost of BI schemes), including:

- **The Winter Fuel Payments**
- **NI State Retirement Pensions paid to those who now live overseas;**

Obtain 'Long-term-projections-pensioner-benefits.pdf', for the forecast for:

- **State Earnings-Related Pension Scheme (SERPS)** and the **State Second Pension (S2P)**

Her Majesty's Revenue and Customs (HMRC)

Access www.gov.uk and search for the following information:

- **Income Tax rates and thresholds;**
- **National Insurance contribution rates and thresholds;** and
- **Working and Child Tax Credit rates and thresholds, Child Benefit and Guardian's Allowance.**

In future, the family element of CTC (£545) will only be available for a child born before 06/04/2017, and the child element is to be limited to two children only.

At all ages, for every £2 that one's income is above £100,000 a year, the Personal Allowance goes down by £1, until the Personal Allowance is zero, ie at income level £125,000 in 2020–21.

Google 'HMRC Table x.y' for the following useful HMRC tables:

- **Table 1.5**: 'Estimated costs of the principal tax expenditures and structural reliefs', HMRC, published December 2018. It is not clear at this stage whether this series will be continued.
- **Table 1.6**: 'Direct effects of illustrative changes in income tax rates' gives changes by 1p in £1 of basic, higher and additional rates of income tax.
- **Table 2.1**: 'Number of individual income taxpayers by marginal rate, gender and age, 1990–91 to 2018–19' gives past data and forecasts.

Other Reputable Sources

- The **National Minimum Wage**, recommended by the Low Pay Commission, comes into force in October each year.
- The **National Living Wage** is merely the National Minimum Wage for people aged 25 or over, and comes into force in April each year.

- The **Living Wage Foundation** recommends hourly rates for in and outside London, which are published on the Monday of the first week of November each year, www.livingwage.org.uk.

Minimum Income Standards (MIS)

The Centre for Research in Social Policy at Loughborough University, provides an annual set of benchmarks using focus groups.

Access www.lboro.ac.uk/research/crsp/mis/results/ and download:

- **'MIS Budget Summaries 2008–2019'**

This can be in either pdf or Excel format, and gives 11 pages of detailed data, each based on a different household configuration. The MIS figures, based on prices in April, are published in early July of that year.

Select Bibliography

A fuller bibliography is available in *A Basic Income Handbook*.

Recent books advocating BI

Torry, Malcolm (2015) *101 Reasons for a Citizen's Income: Arguments for giving everyone some money*, Bristol: Policy Press Shorts.

Bregman, Rutger (2017) *Utopia for Realists: And how we can get there*. London: Bloomsbury

Miller, Annie (2017) *A Basic Income Handbook*, Edinburgh: Luath Press.

Standing Guy (2017) *Basic Income: And How We Can Make It Happen*, London: Penguin Random House.

Van Parijs, Philippe and Vanderborght, Yannick (2017) *Basic Income: A Radical Proposal for a Free Society and a Sane Economy*, Cambridge, MA: Harvard University Press.

Downes, Amy and Lansley, Stewart (eds) (2018) *It's Basic Income: The Global Debate*, Bristol: Policy Press.

Torry, Malcolm (2018a) *Why We Need a Citizen's Basic Income: The desirability, feasibility and implementation of an unconditional income*, Bristol: Policy Press.

Haagh, Louise (2019) *The Case for Universal Basic Income*. Cambridge: Polity Press.

Reports proposing specific schemes for the UK

Painter, Anthony and Thoung, Chris (2015) *Creative citizen, creative state: the principled and pragmatic case for a Universal Basic Income*. London: Royal Society for Arts, www.thersa.org/discover/publications-and-articles/reports/basic-income (accessed 20/06/2018).

Mackenzie, John, Mathers, Siobhan, Mawdsley, Geoff and Payne, Alison (2016) *The Basic Income Guarantee*. Edinburgh: Reform Scotland. www.reformscotland.com/2016/02/the-basic-income-guarantee/ (accessed 20/06/2018).

Reed, Howard and Lansley, Stewart (2016) *Universal Basic Income: An idea whose time has come?* London: Compass.

Miller, Annie (2017) *A Basic Income Handbook*, Edinburgh: Luath Press.

Torry, Malcolm (2017) *A variety of indicators evaluated for two implementation methods for a Citizen's Basic Income*, Euromod Working Paper EM 12/17, Colchester: Institute for Social and Economic Research, www.iser.essex.ac.uk/research/publications/working-papers/euromod/em12-17 (accessed 20/06/2018).

Torry, Malcolm (2018b) *An update, a correction, and an extension, of an evaluation of an illustrative Citizen's Basic Income scheme – addendum to EUROMOD working paper EM12/17*, Colchester: Institute for Social and Economic Research, www.iser.essex.ac.uk/research/publications/working-papers/euromod/em12-17a (accessed 8/03/19).

Painter A., Cooke J., Burbidge I. and Ahmed A. (2019) *A Basic Income for Scotland*, London: The RSA. Available at https://www.thersa.org/globalassets/pdfs/rsa-a-basic-income-for-scotland.pdf.

Standing, Guy (2019) *Piloting Basic Income as Common Dividends*, London: PEF. Available via https://www.progressiveeconomyforum.com/wp-content/uploads/2019/05/PEF_Piloting_Basic_Income_Guy_Standing.pdf.

Lansley, Stewart and Reed, Howard (2019) *Basic Income for All: From Desirability to Feasibility*, London: Compass.

References by some gainsayers

Coote, Anna (2018) 'There are fairer ways to spread prosperity than universal basic income: better alternatives include universal public services and a minimum income guarantee', *New Economics*, 8 February 2018.

Cruddas, Jon and Kibasi, Tom (2016) 'A universal basic mistake: the new fashion for the old idea of a universal basic income is misguided. It's still a bad idea'. *Prospect*, 16 June 2017.

Gough, Ian (2016) 'Potential benefits and pitfalls of a universal basic income', Letter to *The Guardian*, 10 June 2016, www.theguardian.com/politics/2016/jun/10/potential-benefits-and-pitfalls-of-a-universal-basic-income (accessed 20/06/2018).

Hirsch, Donald (2015) *Could a 'Citizen's Income' work?* York: Joseph Rowntree Foundation, 4 March 2015, www.jrf.org.uk/publications/could-citizens-income-work (accessed 20/06/2018).

Kay, John (2017) 'The Basics of Basic Income', *Intereconomics*, 52(2): 69–74.

Piachaud, David (2016) '*Citizen's Income: Rights and Wrongs*', CASE paper 200, Centre for Analysis of Social Exclusion, London: London School of Economics, sticerd.lse.ac.uk/dps/case/cp/casepaper200.pdf (accessed 20/06/2018).

References concerning BI pilot projects

Barclay, Coryn, McLachlan, Julie and Paterson, Mhairi (2019) *Exploring the practicalities of basic income pilots*, Dunfermline: Carnegie UK Trust, www.carnegieuktrust.

org.uk/publications/exploring-the-practicalities-of-a-basic-income-pilot/ (accessed 29/01/19).

Citizen's Basic Income Feasibility Study Steering Group (2019). *Assessing the Feasibility of Citizen's Basic Income Pilots in Scotland: An Interim Report.* Available via https://basicincome.scot.

Davala, Sarath, Jhabvala, Renana, Kapoor Mehta, Soumya, and Standing, Guy (2015) *Basic Income: A Transformative Policy for India*, London: Bloomsbury.

Fairer Fife Commission (2015). *Fairness Matters* (report), www.fifedirect.org.uk/publications/index.cfm?fuseaction=publications.pop&pubid=74F54F0B-0FF8-512C-553C927782FD6B90 (Accessed 7 May 2018).

Forget, Evelyn L. (2012) 'Canada: The Case for Basic Income', in Murray, Matthew C. and Pateman, Carole (eds), *Basic Income Worldwide: Horizons of Reform*. New York: Palgrave Macmillan: 81–101.

Haarman, Claudia and Haarman, Dirk (2008) *Towards a Basic Income Grant for All: Basic Income Grant Pilot Project First Assessment Report*. Namibian Basic Income Grant Coalition, www.bignam.org/BIG_publications.html (accessed 20/06/2018).

Jourdan, Stanislas (2013) 'A Way to Get Healthy: Basic Income Experiments in Canada', Stanislas Jourdan interviews Prof Evelyn Forget. Access the BIEN website, www.basicincome.org and search for 'Jourdan'. (accessed 20/06/2018).

Lum, Zi-Ann (2014) 'A Canadian City Once Eliminated Poverty and Nearly Everyone Forgot About It', *Huffington Post Canada*, 23 December 2014, updated 1 March 2017, www.huffingtonpost.ca/2014/12/23/mincome-in-dauphan-manitoba_n_6335682.html (accessed 20/06/2018).

Tabatabai, H. (2012) 'Iran's Citizen's Income Scheme and its Lessons', *Citizen's Income Newsletter*, issue 2: 2–4.

Widerquist, Karl (2010) 'Viewpoint article: Lessons of the Alaska Dividend', *Citizen's Income Newsletter*, issue 3: 13–15.

Widerquist, Karl (2011) 'Two Memoirs Tell the History of the Alaska Dividend', *Citizen's Income Newsletter*, issue 2: 8–11.

Other recommended reading

Atkinson, Anthony B. (2015) *Inequality: What can be done?* Cambridge, MA: Harvard University Press.

De Wispelaere, Jurgen and Stirton, Lindsay (2008) 'Why Participation Income Might Not Be Such a Great Idea After All', *Citizen's Income Newsletter*, issue 3: 3–8.

Elder-Woodward, Jim and Duffy, Simon (2018) *An Emancipatory Welfare State: How a basic income might underpin the development of human potential*. Sheffield: Centre for Welfare Reform.

Forget, Evelyn (2018) 'Is a basic income good for your health?' Glasgow Centre for Population Health Seminar series no 15, lecture 1, on 18 September 2018. Presentation slides and podcast available via www.gcph.co.uk/publications (accessed 8/3/19).

Jones, Owen (2014) *The Establishment: And how they get away with it*, London: Penguin (Allen Lane).

Martinelli, Luke (2017) *The Fiscal and Distributional Implications of Alternative Universal Basic Income Schemes in the UK*, IPR Working Paper, March 2017, Bath: Institute for Policy Research, www.bath.ac.uk/ipr/policy-briefs/working-papers/the-fiscal-and-distributional-implications-of-alternative-universal-basic-income-schemes-in-the-uk.html (accessed 20/06/2018).

Noguera, José (2018) 'What is the 'net cost' of a basic income? Some conceptual problems'. Paper presented at BIEN Congress 2018, www.basicincome.org/research/ (accessed 6/01/19).

Spicker, Paul (2005) 'Targeting, residual welfare and related concepts: modes of operation in public policy', *Public Administration*, vol. 83, no.2: 345–65.

Spicker, Paul (2017) *What's wrong with Social Security benefits?* Bristol: Policy Press Shorts.

Spicker, Paul (2019) *Some reservations about basic income*, Glasgow: Scottish Universities Insight Institute.

TUC (2016) *Congress Report*, www.tuc.org.uk/sites/default/files/Congress_2016_GPC_Report_Digital.pdf (accessed 8/03/19).

Van Trier, Walter (1995) *Every One a King: An investigation into the meaning and significance of the debate on basic incomes with special reference to three episodes from the British Inter-War experience.* Doctoral thesis. Leuven: Departement Sociologie, Katholiecke Universteit Leuven.

Welfare Charter (2015) 'Welfare launched at TUC Congress 2015',

www.londonunemployedstrategies.com/2015/.../welfare-charter-launched-at-tuc-congress-2015/ (accessed 8/03/19).

Wilkinson, Richard and Pickett, Kate (2009). *The Spirit Level: Why More Equal Societies Almost Always Do Better.* London: Allen Lane/Penguin.

Organisations: information and contacts

The Citizen's Basic Income Network Scotland, CBINS, received its educational charity status (SCIO, no SC046356) in February 2016. It focuses on BI for a more fiscally devolved or independent Scotland. Website: www.cbin.scot.

The Citizen's Basic Income Trust, CBIT, is a long-standing educational charity (CIO no. 1171533) based in London, focusing on UK-wide BI. It started life as the Basic Income Research Group (BIRG) in 1984, and became the Citizen's Income Trust in 1993, before adopting the constitution of a Charitable Incorporated Organisation in 2017 and changing its name once more. It publishes its thrice-yearly *Citizen's Income Newsletter*. Its comprehensive website gives access to an archive of information, including everything that the organisation has ever published.
Website: www.citizensincome.org.

Basic Income UK, BI-UK, is a collective of independent citizens promoting unconditional basic income as a progressive social policy towards an emancipatory welfare state for the UK and beyond. Set up in 2013, while campaigning in the UK for the European Citizens' Initiative for Unconditional Basic Income (ECI on UBI), BI-UK is a network of grassroot groups who are interested in the idea of, and wish to campaign for, a Basic Income in the UK. Website: www.basicincome.org.uk.

The Basic Income Earth Network, BIEN, was set up in Louvain-la-Neuve, Belgium in 1986. It is a network of

national BI groups. Since its inception, BIEN has organised biennial international Congresses, but from 2016 these have become annual events. Papers from some of the congresses are still accessible via its website, www.basicincome.org. Supporters can sign up to receive news by email. With the support of other BI organisations, BIEN set up the e-journal *Basic Income Studies* in 2006, the first, and so far the only, peer-reviewed academic journal dedicated to the subject of BI and the related issues of poverty relief and universal welfare.
www.basicincome.org/research/basic-income-studies/.

Unconditional Basic Income – Europe (UBI–Europe) is an alliance of individuals and organisations from over 25 countries, which developed as a result of organising for ECI on UBI in 2013, with the aim of continuing to promote BI across Europe. www.basicincome-europe.org/ubie/.

A5 leaflets containing compact information about BI can be read on screen or downloaded from www.basicincome-info.org/. The Excel programs for designing and costing your own BI models for Scotland or the UK, as specified in Appendix C above, are also available online here.

What you can do

- Donate time, ideas, skills, energy and money to one or more of the above organisations.
- Become familiar with the arguments for and against a BI scheme, and have some figures at your fingertips.
- Devise schemes for yourself according to your own priorities, and cost them, using different sources of finance, to see what is economically viable.
- Use narrative and personal stories to change people's world view about both what is and what could be. Change hearts and minds.

- Discuss the BI idea with your family and friends.
- Organise talks, discussions and debates within your own spheres of influence.
- Discuss BI with your MP and MSP. Invite them to take part in a debate about BI. Persuade them to support BI pilot project proposals at Westminster and Holyrood.
- Train to become an ambassador via CBINS, and give talks to your local groups and others.

Index

Txx indicates that the subject is part of a table on page xx.
Fyy indicates that the subject is part of a figure on page yy.

AIDS 14, 70, 72
Alaska 64, 67–9, 74, 75, 205, 230
All party parliamentary group 178, 179
Anxiety 27, 31, 44, 51, 56, 84, 100, 153, 211
Assessment 112, 149
   Unit 40, T58, 112, 115, 210, 211
Asylum seekers 94, 212
Atkinson, Anthony B 49, 204, 206, 230
Austerity 154, 181
Automation 30, 45, 151, 154–5, 176, 180, 207, 215, 218
Autonomy 51, T54, 114

Bank account 77, 78, 82, 93, 113, 167
Basic Income
   child 23, 91, 100, 101, 103, 108, 109, 128, 129, 170, 213, 216
   class of income maintenance systems 23, 49, 90
   counter arguments 25, 177, 210
   criticisms of 25, 57, 60–2, 172, 177, 210–9
   design and cost your own scheme 25, 188, 193
   indexation 114
   international 18, 95, 180, 213

Basic Income European/Earth Network (BIEN) 1, 14, 18, 29, 47, 198, 206, 232
Basic Income Research Group (BIRG) 1, 17, 205, 232
Basic Income UK 207, 232
Biometric records 112
Blue Book 14, 39, 108, 134, 187, 220–2
Brexit 180, 181

Canada 202, 205, 229
   Dauphin 8, 64–7
   Ontario 209
Carers 30, 39, 101, 102, T186
Census 77, 112, 168, 220
Centre for Research in Social Policy (CRSP) 225
Childcare
   Costs 45, 105, 213
   Provision 32, 44, 92, 150, 156
Child Poverty Act 2010 40, 95
Child Tax Credit 14, T186, 187, 224
Chronology of basic income
   in the UK 16, 198
   worldwide 69
Citizenship 17, 78, 93
Citizen's Basic Income Network Scotland (CBINS) 1, 14, 17, 28, 85–6, 208, 232, 234

Citizen's Basic Income Trust 1, 14, 28, 198, 205, 232
Citizen's Income Trust 17, 205, 232
Cohabitation rule 43, T54, T58
Compliance 52, T55, 91, 112
Compassion 31, 32, 94, 181, 182, 198
Conditionality 43–4, T58, 61
Control over use of own time 51, T59, 61, 149, 151
Co-operatives 153
Covid-19 26, 209
Costs
  gross cost of a BI 127
  net cost of a BI 127, 231
  sum of gross transfers 105, T108, T109, 127, 130, 169, T188, T189, T194
  sum of net transfers 24, 127
  will it cost too much? 173, 215
Council Tax Reduction / Support 14, 92, 187
Couples 40, 43, T54, 60, 100, 101, T186, 211

Department for Work and Pensions (DWP) 14, 95, 111, 131, 222–3
Disability benefits 34, T59, 91, 101, 105, T106, 107, 110, 124, 127, 192
Disabled people 34, 65, 78, 92, 101, 165
  costs incurred by 213
  needs of 91
Discrimination T54, T55
Donne, John 33
Douglas, Major C.H. 202

Earnings disregard (EDR) T128, T129, 131

Economies of scale
  Household 14, 60, 100, 211
Eligibility criteria 51, 93, 94, 112, 165, 212
Emancipation 51, 52, 53, T54, 57, T59, 64, 92, 151, 217
Empowerment 53, T54, 78
Equivalised 95, 97, T186, 223
European Citizens' Initiative 17, 206, 232
European Union (EU) 206
  Referendum 180-1
  official poverty benchmark, *see* poverty

Feasibility 162, 177, 208–9, 218, 226, 228
Fife 85, 229
Financial crisis 69, 175, 181
Financial dependent 41
Financial dependence 53, T55, 211
Financially vulnerable adults 101, 102
Finland 83–5, 167, 208
Forget, Evelyn 34, 65, 66, 229, 230
Free-riders T59, 214

General Election 26, 178, 208
George, Henry 201
Gift Aid 123
Gini coefficient 35
Glasgow 17, 85, 202
Globalisation 175, 180
Gordian knot 45
Government expenditure 120, 123, 124, 125
Green Party of England & Wales 176, 207, 208

Heath Edward, MP 204
Her Majesty's Revenue and
  Customs (HMRC) 14, 111, 112,
  187, 223–4
Holyrood 31, 86, 208, 234
Households Below Average
  Income (HBAI) 14, 95, 131, 222
Housing
  benefit 14, T59, 92, 96, 105, 107,
    T121, 127, T184, 187, 213
  costs 14, 23, 92, 95, 99, 150, 213
  policy 92, 154, 213
  social 32
Hypothecation (ring-fencing) 125

Implementation
  gradual approach 25, 101, 114,
    142, 145, 151, 176
  sector approach 115
Income sources 99
Income maintenance systems
  23, 32, 49, 57, 82, 90, 91, 154
Income tax
  Avoidance 125
  breakeven points 136, 140, 144
  evasion 112, 116, 127, 171
  Progressive 23, 35, 52, T59, 104,
    130, 151, 154, 177, 182
  proportionate (flat tax) 24, 126,
    130
India 76–82, 168, 180, 206, 229
Industrial democracy T55, T59,
  149
Inequality of income T55, 200
Inflation 64, 77, 97, 103, 119, 154,
  216–7
Integrity 1, 31
Iran 72–5, 206, 230

Jones, Owen 123, 230
Justice 31–2, 60, 117, 181–2,
  199–200

Kenya 86–7
Korea, Republic of 87

Labour
  demand for 151, 155, 160
  reservation wage T55, 148, 152
  supply 148, 158
Land Value Tax 117, 119, 201
Liberal Party 203, 204–5
Living Wage Foundation 152,
  T186, 225

McDonnell, John, MP 208
McKay, Ailsa 17, 206
Manifesto 178, 204, 208
Marginal deduction rate (MDR)
  14, 42, T55, 126, 148, 151
Marriage 40, 41, 43, 56, 159
Meade, James E 16, 202, 203, 204
Means-tested benefits 42, 52, 117,
  164, 187
Microsimiulation 25, 136, 157–59,
  161, 166, 177
Migration 93–5, 180, 212–3
Milner, Dennis 201–2
Mincome project 64–7, 205, 229
Minimum Income Standards
  (MIS) 14, 98, 99, 179, 225,

Namibia 70-2, 180, 206, 220
National Dividend 16, 202
National Insurance Primary
  Threshold T121, 126, T185
National Living Wage 15, 43, 152,
  215, 224

National Minimum Wage 15, 224
Natural resources 33, 61, 67, 118, 213
Negative income tax (NIT) 15, 16, 111
Neoliberal 181
New Zealand 123
Non-Profit Institutions Serving Households (NPISHs) 221-2
Nordic countries 44, 112, 126, 151, 174, 216
Nutrition 71-2, 78-9, 81, 159

Paine, Thomas 33, 200
Painter, Anthony 208, 226, 227
Panacea 23
Parallel systems 91, 92, 105, 213
Participation Income 19, 49, T59, 83, 230
Pay As You Earn (PAYE) 15, 111, 125
Payroll tax 127
Pension Credit 15, 102, T103, 106, 108, 112, 128, 137, 144, T186
Pilot projects 64, 209, 228
   phases 162
Political process 25, 175
Poor Law 199
Poverty
   benchmark 46, 92, 96, 99, 100, 158, 181
   EU 40, 95, T96, 100, 102, T103, T110, 179, 197
   MIS 98, T110, 179
   proposed alternative 97, 98, 135, 142, 145, 179
   floor 17, T110, T192
Prisoners 34, 94
Productivity 52, T55, 64, 78, 80, 82, 156, 160
Prosperity 96, 114, 179, 180

Quaker 1, 199, 201
Quantitative Easing 119

Reciprocity T59, 61, 74, 213
Redistribution of income 37, 153, 154, 217
   vertical, the case for 35-6
Relationships 45, 53, 94, 182
   household 42, T54, 56, T58, T59, 60, 71, 158
   workplace T55, T59, 149
Reservation wage, *see* labour
Residency conditions 93
Rich people
   giving a BI to T59, 60, 211-2,
   who are they? 36-7
   will emigrate? 173, 216

Sanctions 43, 44, T54, T58 149
Scottish feasibility study 85, 86, 176, 208, 209, 229
Scottish Green Party 118, 207
Scottish mace 31
Scottish National Accounts Project (SNAP) 15, 222
Scottish National Party (SNP) 208
Scottish Parliament 31, 207, 209
Scottish Social Security Committee 208
Seigniorage 119
Self Employed Women's Association (SEWA) 76
Social Credit 16, 202
Social dividend 16, 202-3, 204
Social Security systems (*see* income maintenance systems)
Something for nothing 61, 213-4
Sovereign Wealth Fund 68, 74, 118, 119

Spicker, Paul 19, 28, 44, 104, 231
Standing, Guy 18, 82, 206, 208, 209, 226, 227
State Bonus 16, 201-2,
State Earnings Related Pension Scheme (SERPS) 15, 103, 223
State Retirement Pension 15, 39, 102, 105, T186, 223
State Second Pension (S2P) 15, 223
Stigma 34, 41, 44, T54, T55, T58
Stress 31, 34, 44, 52, T54, T59, 100, 101, 149, 153, 169, 181, 211
Students 56, 94
Switzerland 208

Targeting 42, 49, T54, T55, T58, 60, 212, 231
  and segregation 41, T58, 212
Tax expenditures 119, T121, 123, 141, T185, 224
Tax loopholes 23, 25, 123, 125, 151, 171
Taxes, UK
  Corporation tax 117, 118, 119, T121, 155, T185
  Sales 118, 155
  Transactions 118
  VAT 15, 117-9, T121
Technological change 151
Torry, Malcolm 115, 206, 208, 226, 227
Trades unions 149, 151, 174, 177
Transport 32, 79, 80, 107, 156, 168

Unconditionality 49, 53, 61, 149, 167
UNICEF 76
Universal Basic Services 175, 217
Universal Credit 15, 106, 111, 126, 176, T186, 187, 213, 219

Universal Declaration of Human Rights (UDHR) 33, 203
Universality 49, 53, 60, 74, 113
Utopian schemes 210
USA 16, 118,
  Alaska 67
  income maintenance experiments 204

Values 1, 30, 31, T54, T59, 62, 199, 214
Van Parijs, Philippe 1, 18, 98, 118, 206, 226
Van Trier, Walter 202, 206, 231
Viability 124, 162, 176, 210

Wage protection 151, 214-5
Wage rates 94, 158
  changes in 42, 44, T55, T59, 149, 152, 180, 214, 217
  net 41, T55
Water 79, 118
Well-being 33, 52, 53, T54, 64, 78, 79, 82, 152, 153, 203
Westminster 14, 176, 208, 217, 234
Widerquist, Karl 68-9, 230
Wilkinson and Pickett 36, 207, 231
Wisdom 31, 69
Withdrawal taper 42, 92, 148
Women's lives 38, 71
Work
  for-pay 30, 41, 45, 52, 53, T54, T55, T59, 61, 83, 158, 182, 214
  unpaid T55, T59, 61, 173, 214
World Bank 33, 206

Y-BAR 98
  Definition 15, 130

Luath Press Limited
committed to publishing well written books worth reading

LUATH PRESS takes its name from Robert Burns, whose little collie Luath (*Gael.*, swift or nimble) tripped up Jean Armour at a wedding and gave him the chance to speak to the woman who was to be his wife and the abiding love of his life. Burns called one of 'The Twa Dogs' Luath after Cuchullin's hunting dog in Ossian's *Fingal*. Luath Press was established in 1981 in the heart of Burns country, and now resides a few steps up the road from Burns' first lodgings on Edinburgh's Royal Mile.

Luath offers you distinctive writing with a hint of unexpected pleasures.

Most bookshops in the UK, the US, Canada, Australia, New Zealand and parts of Europe either carry our books in stock or can order them for you. To order direct from us, please send a £sterling cheque, postal order, international money order or your credit card details (number, address of cardholder and expiry date) to us at the address below. Please add post and packing as follows: UK – £1.00 per delivery address; overseas surface mail – £2.50 per delivery address; overseas airmail – £3.50 for the first book to each delivery address, plus £1.00 for each additional book by airmail to the same address. If your order is a gift, we will happily enclose your card or message at no extra charge.

Luath Press Limited
543/2 Castlehill
The Royal Mile
Edinburgh EH1 2ND
Scotland

Telephone: 0131 225 4326 (24 hours)
email: sales@luath.co.uk
Website: www.luath.co.uk